STUDENT UNIT GU[IDE]

AS Biology UNIT 2

AQA Specification A

Module 2: Making Use of Biology

Steve Potter

Philip Allan Updates
Market Place
Deddington
Oxfordshire
OX15 0SE

Tel: 01869 338652
Fax: 01869 337590
e-mail: sales@philipallan.co.uk
www.philipallan.co.uk

ISBN 0 86003 487 9

This Guide has been written specifically to support students preparing for the AQA Specification A AS Biology Unit 2 examination. The content has been neither approved nor endorsed by AQA and remains the sole responsibility of the author.

Typeset by Magnet Harlequin, Oxford
Printed by Information Press, Eynsham, Oxford

P00058

Contents

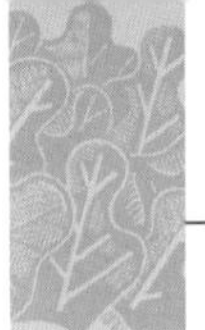

Introduction

About this guide

This guide is written to help you to prepare for the Unit 2 examination of the AQA Biology Specification A. Unit 2 examines the content of **Module 2: Making Use of Biology**, and forms part of the AS assessment. It will also form part of the A2 assessment with some of the material being re-examined in the end of A2 synoptic examination.

This Introduction provides guidance on revision, together with advice on approaching the examination itself.

The Content Guidance section gives a point-by-point description of all the facts you need to know and concepts you need to understand for Module 2. Although each fact and concept is explained where necessary, you must be prepared to use other resources in your preparation.

The Question and Answer section shows you the sort of questions you can expect in the unit test. It would be impossible to give examples of every kind of question in one book, but these should give you a flavour of what to expect. Each question has been attempted by two candidates, Candidate A and Candidate B. Their answers, along with the examiner's comments, should help you to see what you need to do to score a good mark — and how you can easily *not* score a mark even though you probably understand the biology.

What can I assume about the guide?

You can assume that:

- the topics described in the Content Guidance section correspond to those in the specification
- the basic facts you need to know are stated clearly
- the major concepts you need to understand are explained
- the questions at the end of the guide are similar in style to those that will appear in the unit test
- the answers supplied are genuine answers — not concocted by the author
- the standard of the marking is broadly equivalent to the standard that will be applied to your answers

What can I *not* assume about the guide?

You *must not* assume that:

- every last detail has been covered
- the diagrams used will be the same as those used in a unit test (they may be more or less detailed, seen from a different angle etc.)

- the way in which the concepts are explained is the *only* way in which they can be presented in an examination (often concepts are presented in an unfamiliar situation)
- the range of question types presented is exhaustive (examiners are always thinking of new ways to test a topic)

So how should I use this guide?

The guide lends itself to a number of uses throughout your course — it is not *just* a revision aid. Because the Content Guidance is laid out in sections that correspond to those of the specification for Module 2, you can:

- use it to check that your notes cover the material required by the specification
- use it to identify strengths and weaknesses
- use it as a reference for homework and internal tests
- use it during your revision to prepare 'bite-sized' chunks of related material, rather than being faced with a file full of notes

The Question and Answer section can be used to:

- identify the terms used by examiners in questions and what they expect of you
- familiarise yourself with the style of questions you can expect
- identify the ways in which marks are lost as well as the ways in which they are gained

Preparing for the Unit 2 test

Preparation for examinations is a very personal thing. Different people prepare, equally successfully, in very different ways. The key is being totally honest about what actually *works* for *you*. This is *not* necessarily the same as the style you would like to adopt. It is no use preparing to a background of rock music if this distracts you.

Whatever your style, you must have a plan. Sitting down the night before the examination with a file full of notes and a textbook does not constitute a revision plan — it is just desperation — and you must not expect a great deal from it. Whatever your personal style, there are a number of things you *must* do and a number of other things you *could* do.

Things you *must* do

- Leave yourself enough time to cover *all* the material.
- Make sure that you actually *have* all the material to hand (use this book as a basis).
- Identify weaknesses early in your preparation so that you have time to do something about them.
- Familiarise yourself with the terminology used in examination questions (see p. 6).

Things you *could* do to help you learn

- Copy selected portions of your notes.
- Write a precis of your notes which includes all the key points.

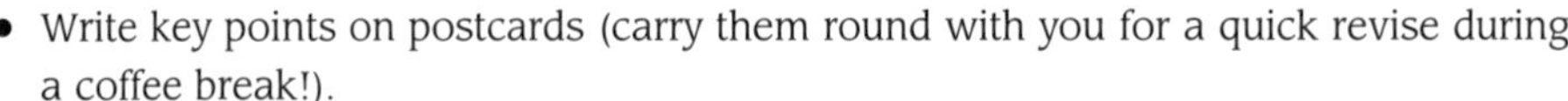

- Write key points on postcards (carry them round with you for a quick revise during a coffee break!).
- Discuss a topic with a friend also studying the same course.
- Try to explain a topic to someone *not* on the course.
- Practise examination questions on the topic.

Approaching the unit test

Terms used in examination questions

You will be asked precise questions in the examinations, so you can save a lot of valuable time as well as ensuring you score as many marks as possible by knowing what is expected. Terms most commonly used are explained below.

Describe

This means exactly what it says — 'tell me about...' — and you should not need to explain why.

Explain

Here you must give biological reasons for *why* or *how* something is happening.

Complete

You must finish off a diagram, graph, flow chart or table.

Draw/plot

This means that you must construct some type of graph. For this, make sure that:

- you choose a scale that makes good use of the graph paper (if a scale is not given) and does not leave all the plots tucked away in one corner
- plot an appropriate type of graph — if both variables are continuous variables, then a line graph is usually the most appropriate; if one is a discrete variable, then a bar chart is appropriate
- plot carefully using a sharp pencil and draw lines accurately

From the...

This means that you must use only information in the diagram/graph/photograph or other forms of data.

Name

This asks you to give the name of a structure/molecule/organism etc.

Suggest

This means 'give a plausible biological explanation for' — it is often used when testing understanding of concepts in an unfamiliar situation.

Compare

In this case you have to give similarities *and* differences between...

Calculate

This means add, subtract, multiply, divide (do some kind of sum!) and show how you got your answer — *always show your working!*

When you finally open the test paper, it can be quite a stressful moment. You may not recognise the diagram or graph used in question 1. It can be quite demoralising to attempt a question at the start of an examination if you are not feeling very confident about it. So:

- *do not* begin to write as soon as you open the paper
- *do not* answer question 1 first, just because it is printed first (the examiner did not sequence the questions with your particular favourites in mind)
- *do* scan *all* the questions before you begin to answer any
- *do* identify those questions about which you feel most confident
- *do answer first* those questions about which you feel most confident regardless of order in the paper
- *do read the question carefully* — if you are asked to explain, then explain, don't just describe
- *do* take notice of the mark allocation and don't supply the examiner with all your knowledge of osmosis if there is only 1 mark allocated (similarly, you will have to come up with four ideas if 4 marks are allocated)
- *do* try to stick to the point in your answer (it is easy to stray into related areas that will not score marks and will use up valuable time)
- *do* take care with
  - drawings — you will not be asked to produce complex diagrams, but those you do produce must resemble the subject
  - labelling — label lines *must touch* the part you are required to identify; if they stop short or pass through the part, you will lose marks
  - graphs — draw *small* points if you are asked to plot a graph and join the plots with ruled lines or, if specifically asked for, a line or smooth curve of best fit through all the plots
- *do try* to answer *all* the questions

Content Guidance

This section is a guide to the content of **Module 2: Making Use of Biology**. The main areas of this module are:

- Isolation of microbial enzymes and their use in biotechnology
- The cell cycle, mitosis and meiosis
- Structure and functions of DNA and RNA
- Genetic engineering
- Using biotechnology in forensic science
- Crop production
- Control of reproduction in humans and domestic animals

You should think of this section as a 'translation' of the specification from 'examiner speak' into more user-friendly language. At the same time I have tried to be very precise in describing exactly what is required of you. This is done for each area in the module under the headings described below.

Key facts you must know

These are exactly what you might think: a summary of all the basic knowledge that you must be able to recall. All the actual knowledge has been broken down into a number of small facts that you must learn. This means that the list of 'Key facts' for some topics is quite long. However, this approach makes quite clear *everything* you need to know about the topic. You need to learn the key facts for a topic before you try to understand the key concepts.

Key concepts you must understand

These are a little different: whereas you can learn facts, you must *understand* these ideas or concepts. You can know the actual words that describe a concept like mitosis, or DNA replication, but you will not be able to use this information unless you really understand what is going on. Once you genuinely understand a concept, you will probably not have to learn it again. I have given brief explanations of all the major concepts, but you must be prepared to refer to your notes and textbooks or ask your teacher for a fuller explanation.

What the examiners will expect you to be able to do

In this part, I have tried to give you an insight into the minds of the examiners who will set and mark your examination papers. Obviously, they may ask you to recall any of the basic knowledge or explain any of the key concepts; but they may well do more than that. Examiners think up questions where the concepts you understand are in a different setting or context from the one(s) you are familiar with. I have tried, in this section, to prepare you for the sorts of questions they might ask. This can never be exhaustive, but it will give you a good idea of what can be asked of you. Bear in mind that examiners will often set individual questions that involve knowledge and understanding of more than one section. The sample questions in the Question and Answer section of this book will help you to practise this skill.

After each topic there is a short paragraph marked 'Links'. While not crucial to the understanding of any of the biology, this should give you some idea of how the biology you are learning will be related to other topics that you may meet in other modules.

The isolation of microbial enzymes and their use in biotechnology

The isolation of microbial enzymes

Key facts you must know

Some enzymes are **intracellular enzymes**. These are produced inside living cells and only catalyse reactions inside these cells. The enzymes catalysing the reactions of protein synthesis are examples of intracellular enzymes.

Other enzymes are **extracellular enzymes**. These are produced within living cells but are secreted by the cells and catalyse reactions outside the cell. The amylases, secreted by cells in the pancreas and salivary glands, are examples of extracellular enzymes.

Modern biotechnology allows microbial enzymes to be isolated for use in industrial processes. The main stages in the extraction of an extracellular microbial enzyme are shown in the flow chart below.

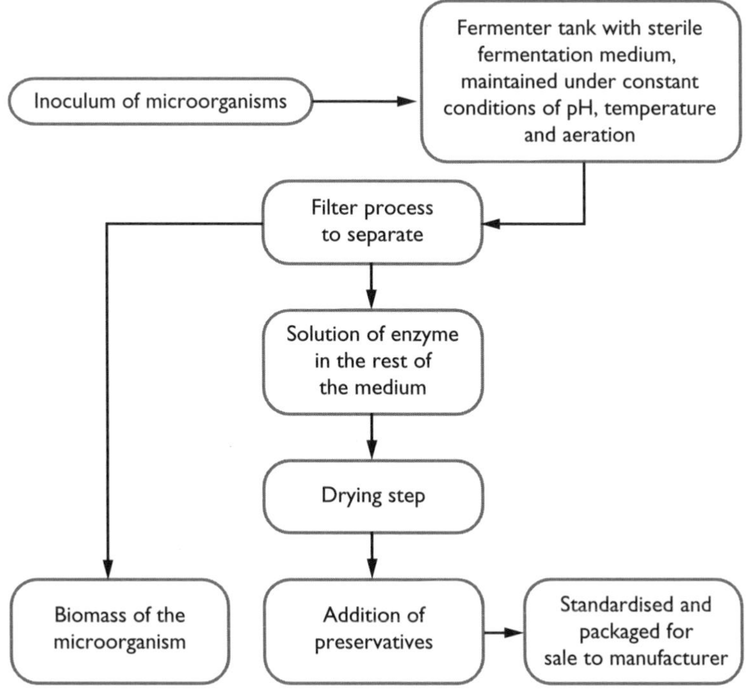

When intracellular enzymes are being extracted, the downstream processing is more difficult, as the microbial cells must be broken open and the enzyme separated from a mix of cellular components.

Tip Make sure that you know and understand the jargon! Terms like 'culture medium', 'aseptic conditions' and 'downstream processing' frequently appear in examination papers. Also, be aware that 'downstream processing' to isolate and purify the enzyme can account for as much as 80% of the total cost of the process.

Key concepts you must understand

The use of a purified enzyme (rather than the whole microorganism that produces it) in a biotechnological process can have several advantages, including:

- only one reaction need be considered and conditions can be 'optimised' more easily (with a whole microorganism, many metabolic reactions are taking place, each with differing requirements)
- the reactants are used to produce only the desired product (with a microorganism, a significant amount is used to produce microbial biomass)
- as there is only one reaction and one product, downstream processing (to isolate and purify the product) will be less complex and therefore less expensive

The use of enzymes in biotechnological processes

Key facts you must know

Enzymes are increasingly being used as catalysts in manufacturing processes for the following reasons:

- they can catalyse reactions at low temperatures — this saves energy (and money) that would otherwise be needed to heat the reactants to very high temperatures
- enzymes are specific and catalyse only one reaction, so fewer by-products are made and purification is easier
- they are very efficient — each enzyme molecule can catalyse the production of many thousands of product molecules per second (enzymes have a high **turnover rate**)
- they are cheaper than many inorganic catalysts

Because of their specificity, they are often used in **biosensors** — devices used to detect one particular substance (e.g. glucose, cholesterol, urea, penicillin and even heroin).

Some enzymes are more **thermostable** than normal enzymes (they can withstand higher temperatures without denaturing). These can be used at higher temperatures than ordinary enzymes, which allow reactions to proceed even faster.

Enzymes can be **immobilised**, for example in alginate beads or in a cellulose fibre matrix.

Biosensors: key facts you must know

Biosensors make use of reactions catalysed by enzymes to generate either a colour change or a small electrical signal. The colour change or electrical signal is only produced in response to the specific reaction that the enzyme catalyses. The intensity of the colour or the size of the electrical signal produced is usually in proportion to the concentration of a particular substrate, and so the biosensor can measure the concentration of this substrate.

Biosensors producing a colour change in a dye (e.g. Clinistix strips in which glucose causes a colourless dye to change colour) give a 'one-off' indication of the concentration of a substance, but are usually easy to use.

Those producing a small electrical signal that can be continuously recorded and displayed are useful for monitoring changes in the concentration of a substance over a period of time (although they are less convenient to use).

To test for glucose, we could use the Benedict's test, a Clinistix strip, or a biosensor that produces a voltage change in response to detecting glucose. The biosensors have several advantages over conventional biochemical tests:

Benedict's test	Clinistix strip	Biosensor producing a voltage change
Detects all reducing sugars	Detects only glucose	Detects only glucose
Concentrations not easily judged	Concentrations easily judged	Concentrations precisely judged
Continuous monitoring is not possible	Continuous monitoring is not possible	Continuous monitoring is possible
Difficult to detect very low concentrations accurately	Detection of low concentrations is possible	Detection of very low concentrations is possible

The enzymes in the biosensors make the testing specific, precise and reliable. The specificity is due to the precise **conformation** of the active site of the enzyme.

Testing is sensitive because enzymes form complexes with their substrates in very low concentrations.

Thermostable enzymes: key facts you must know

Thermostable enzymes retain their tertiary structure at temperatures that would denature most enzymes.

Raising the temperature of a reaction increases the rate of the reaction by increasing the number of collisions between reacting molecules. In enzyme-controlled reactions, more enzyme–substrate complexes are formed per second as a result of increased collisions. Reaction rates double (approximately) for every 10°C rise in temperature.

Tip **If an enzyme can be used that has an optimum of 70°C, rather than the more usual 30°C, the reaction could be 16 times faster. This means 16 times as much product per minute to a manufacturer. Will the increased heating costs be too much to offset the increased productivity? That is a question for the production engineers.**

Washing powder enzymes often show some degree of thermostability. They can digest stains at moderate temperatures of 30–50°C. This reduces the amount of heating required.

Immobilised enzymes: key facts you must know

Immobilised enzymes are held in some insoluble support material which fixes the enzyme in place. Many ordinary enzymes can be immobilised in alginate beads, or by other means. Immobilising enzymes makes continuous production processes possible.

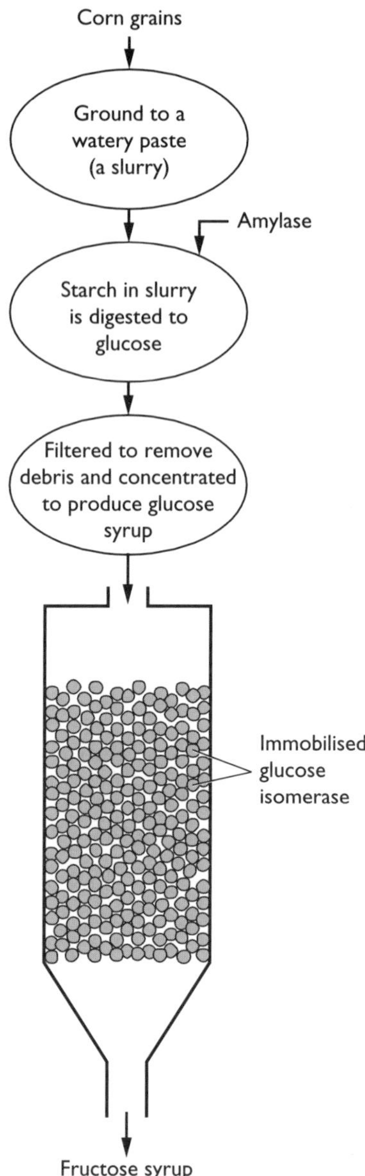

Tip **In a continuous enzyme-controlled production process, the immobilised enzymes are often contained in a 'tower' and the reactants allowed to flow over them. The flow rate of the reactants (which affects the substrate concentration) and other factors (such as temperature and pH), are carefully controlled to optimise conditions for the process. As a result, the rate of catalysis by the enzymes is near maximum and there is very little contamination of the product. Downstream processing to purify the product is less expensive.**

One product made using immobilised enzymes is fructose syrup (used as a sweetener for the food industry).

Using immobilised enzymes has several advantages over using free enzymes:

- the product will not be contaminated by the enzyme, which makes downstream processing less expensive
- it increases the enzymes' stability at higher temperatures and extremes of pH by strengthening bonds that maintain the tertiary structure
- the enzymes can be used through many cycles of the production process before they need replacing

- the enzymes can be used in continuous production processes (which reduces the running costs as the process does not have to be continually stopped) — the product is extracted and purified, the fermenter refilled and the process restarted

One disadvantage in using immobilised enzymes is that some immobilisation processes result in a reduction in enzyme activity. The substrate must collide with the enzyme and, if it is entrapped in an alginate bead, this is not as easy!

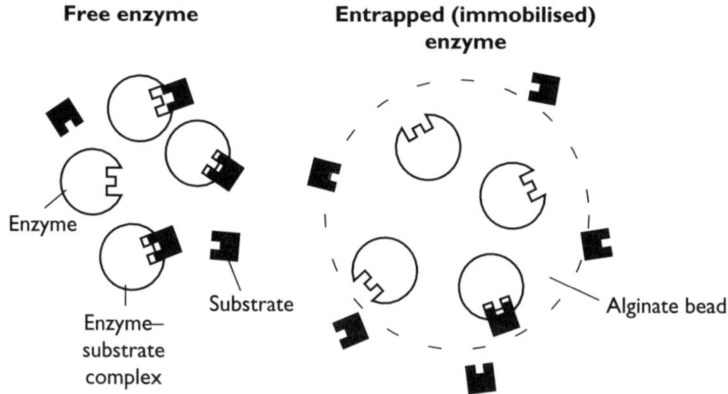

Also, immobilisation is expensive. This cost must be set against the gains from reduced running costs of the continuous production process made possible by immobilisation.

What the examiners will expect you to be able to do

- Recall any of the key facts.
- Explain any of the key concepts.
- Interpret information (including diagrams of fermenters and graphs of production rates) concerning the isolation of microbial enzymes, and comment on how the procedures may or may not optimise the production of enzyme. This could include:
  - commenting on how factors like pH, temperature and oxygenation could affect the productivity in the example given
  - calculating production rates by reading from a graph or from supplied data
  - sketching a new graph to show likely production rates given new conditions, such as an increase in temperature or a decrease in nutrient availability
  - suggesting why certain nutrients (such as amino acids and sugars) are included in the nutrient medium
- Quote one or two examples of the uses of biosensors.
- Compare the rate of reaction of a thermostable enzyme and an ordinary enzyme.
- Deduce whether or not an enzyme is thermostable.
- Suggest possible advantages and disadvantages in using a thermostable enzyme in a particular process specified in the question.
- From data given, comment on the efficiency of a process using immobilised enzymes.

- Predict and explain the likely effect on a continuous production process of changing the flow rate of the reactants.
- From data given, compare and contrast production by a continuous process (using immobilised enzymes) and batch production (using free enzymes).

Links The commercial applications of enzymes are referred to several times in this module and the principles discussed here may be tested in other contexts. Production of specific products could be linked to other modules. Examples include biosensors used by diabetics to monitor glucose levels in blood (Module 5).

The cell cycle, mitosis and meiosis

The cell cycle

Key facts you must know

The cell cycle describes the sequence of events that occur as a cell grows, and prepares for and finally undergoes cell division by mitosis.

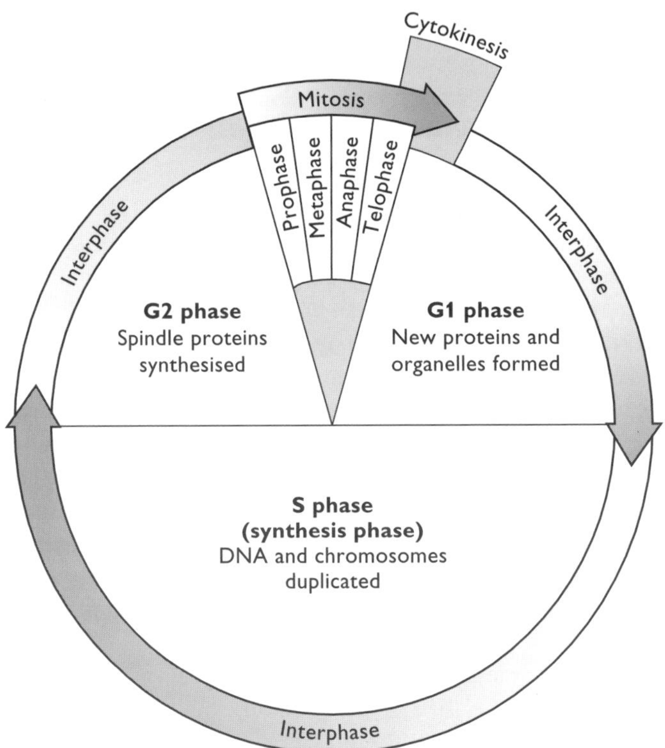

The phases of the cell cycle are as follows:

- **G1 phase** — during this phase, the newly formed cell is comparatively small and starts to produce proteins and new organelles and begins to increase in size
- **S phase** — cell enlargement continues, the DNA of the cells replicates and each chromosome becomes a pair of chromatids joined by a centromere
- **G2 phase** — the spindle proteins needed for cell division are synthesised
- **mitosis** — equal numbers of chromosomes are moved to opposite ends of the cell where each group forms a new nucleus
- **cytokinesis** — the cell divides into two new cells

Some cells complete the cell cycle many times. They must divide repeatedly to form cells for new growth or to replace damaged cells. Examples include:

- cells in the bone marrow which produce red and white blood cells
- epithelial cells lining the intestine which replace those cells lost by being scraped off by food materials passing through the gut
- cells near the tip of a root or shoot

Cells that go through the cell cycle repeatedly are usually relatively unspecialised cells. Specialised cells often have a reduced capacity for cell division. For example, nerve cells, once formed, cannot divide again.

Key concepts you must understand

The amount of DNA in the cell and the volume of the cell change throughout the cycle.

The DNA content doubles during the S phase as it replicates. It then returns to the normal level during cytokinesis as each newly formed cell receives half the chromosomes (and therefore half the DNA).

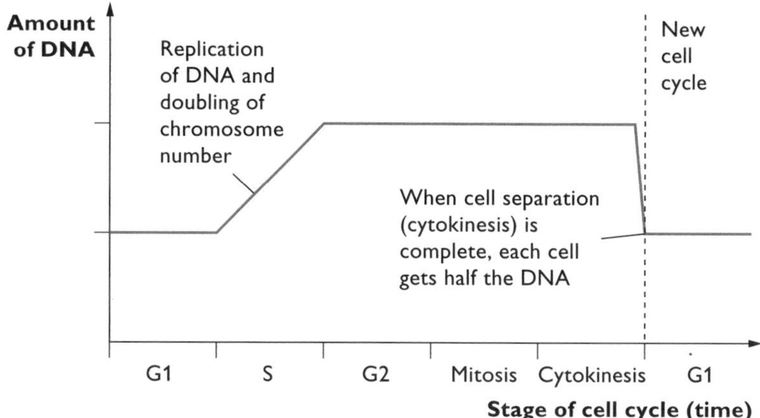

The volume increases steadily through G1, S and G2 as more and more proteins and cytoplasm are made. It remains static during mitosis and then the cell volume halves during cytokinesis as the cell divides into two.

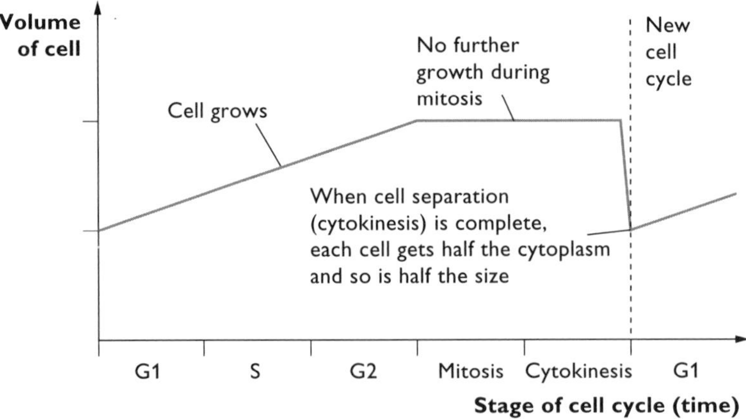

Specialised cells (like nerve cells), once formed, enter the G1 phase, grow to full size and then remain in this state without progressing to the S or G2 phase.

Mitosis

Key facts you must know

Mitosis results in two cells being formed with the same number and type of chromosomes as each other and as the parent cell that formed them. They are genetically identical and so form a **clone** of cells.

The process is divided into four key stages: (1) **prophase**, (2) **metaphase**, (3) **anaphase** and (4) **telophase**.

Tip You do *not* need to know anything at all about the subdivisions of prophase.

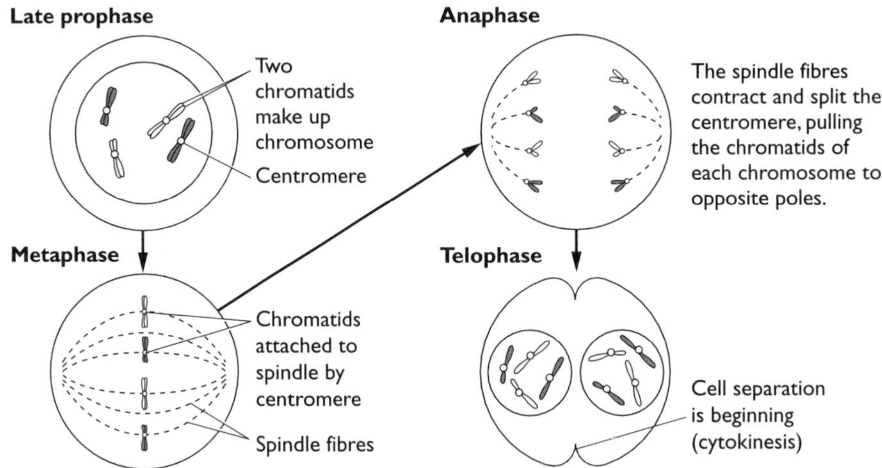

Stage of mitosis	Main events
Prophase	Chromosomes coil and become visible as double structures. Each is called a **chromatid**. (During interphase, the DNA replicated and from one **chromosome**, two identical **sister chromatids** were formed.) They are held together by a **centromere**. The nuclear envelope starts to break down.
Metaphase	The spindle forms. The centromeres attach the chromatids to the spindle fibres so that they lie across the middle of the spindle.
Anaphase	The spindle fibres contract and pull the sister chromatids to opposite poles of the cell. Once the chromatids have been separated, they are called chromosomes again.
Telophase	The spindle fibres are broken down. The two groups of chromosomes group together at each pole and a nuclear envelope forms around each. The chromosomes uncoil and cannot be seen as individual structures.

Key concepts you must understand

Strictly, mitosis describes the division of the chromosomes, *not* of the whole cell. The division of the cell is called **cytokinesis**.

The 46 chromosomes in nearly all human cells are, in fact, 23 pairs called **homologous pairs**. One chromosome from each pair is paternal in origin (from the father) and the other is maternal in origin (from the mother).

Cells with pairs of all the homologous chromosomes like this are called **diploid** cells. The diploid condition is sometimes written as ***2n*** — '*n*' is the number of different chromosomes and there are two (a homologous pair) of each.

Homologous chromosomes carry genes for the same features in the same sequence, although they might not carry the same **alleles** (versions) of these genes.

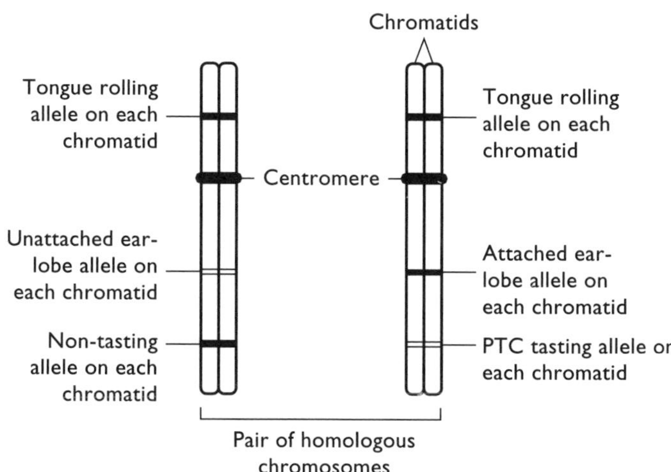

Homologous chromosomes are the same size and shape because they carry the same genes in the same sequence. The sister chromatids formed during interphase *always carry the same alleles of the genes* because of the semi-conservative replication of DNA in the original chromosome.

The cells formed by mitosis are genetically identical because each receives one chromatid from each pair of sister chromatids (by the time it enters the new cell it is called a chromosome again).

Tip So what *is* all this about chromosomes and chromatids? A chromosome usually contains just *one* molecule of DNA and some protein molecules (mainly histones) bound to it. The diagrams show what happens to a chromosome during the S phase of interphase.

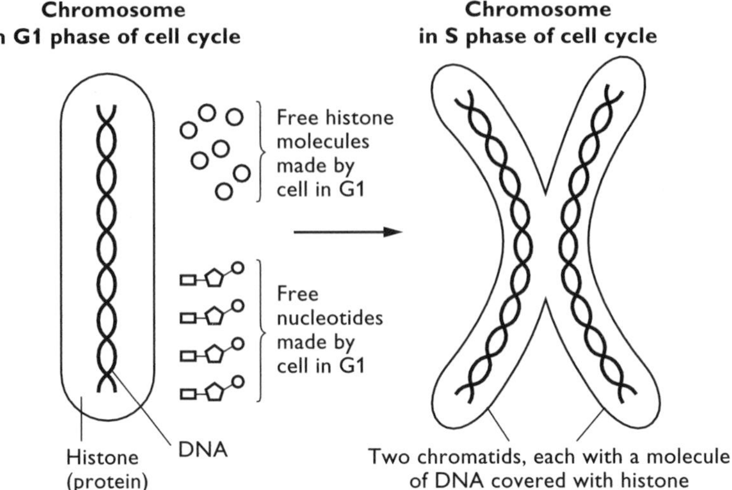

Each of the two structures is like a chromosome since it contains DNA and proteins. But chromosomes don't normally join together, so we call these structures with one DNA molecule **chromatids** and the whole double structure is still a **chromosome**. Once they have separated during mitosis, the chromatids are chromosomes again!

Following fertilisation, the zygote is 'copied' repeatedly by mitosis so that all the body cells are genetically identical. This underlines the importance of mitosis in life cycles.

Meiosis

Key facts you must know

- Meiosis produces cells that show genetic variation.
- Meiosis halves the chromosome number in cells (in humans from 46 to 23). The cells formed by meiosis are usually sex cells.
- There are two cell divisions involved in meiosis.

- Meiosis produces cells that contain only one chromosome from each homologous pair. Such cells are called **haploid** cells. The haploid condition is sometimes written as '*n*'.

Tip You do not need to know all the details of meiosis for AS! But you *do* need to know an outline of the process and understand its importance in life cycles.

Key concepts you must understand

Production of haploid gametes (sex cells) is a necessary part of a life cycle so that when fertilisation occurs, the normal diploid number is restored.

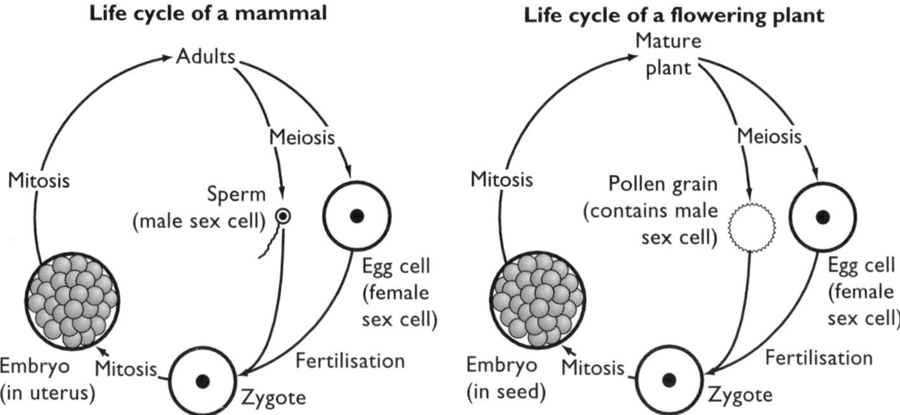

Tip In an exam question, diagrams like those above often include chromosome numbers. Meiosis can be identified by the halving of the chromosome number.

What the examiners will expect you to be able to do

- Recall any of the key facts.
- Explain any of the key concepts.
- Be able to sequence drawings showing cells in various stages of mitosis.
- Compare and contrast meiosis and mitosis.
- Interpret graphs giving information about features of the cell cycle such as cell volume, DNA content and distance of chromosomes from the poles of a cell.
- Recognise from drawings/photographs the various stages of the cell cycle.
- Interpret diagrams of unfamiliar life cycles to identify stages where meiosis and mitosis are taking place.
- From information given about unfamiliar life cycles, deduce the number of chromosomes per cell at various stages of the cycle.

Links An understanding of meiosis is crucial to the understanding of the mechanisms of inheritance. Meiosis in sexual reproduction is a source of genetic variation, which is essential to the process of evolution.

The structure and functions of DNA and RNA

This section looks at the structure and functions of nucleic acids. It is concerned, in particular, with the way in which DNA replicates itself and also the way in which it controls protein synthesis. By controlling protein synthesis, DNA controls the synthesis of enzymes and so, indirectly, controls metabolic pathways within an organism. The products of these metabolic pathways influence the physical appearance (the phenotype) of the organism.

The structure of DNA and RNA

Key facts you must know

- DNA and RNA are **nucleic acids** built from **nucleotides**. Because DNA and RNA contain many nucleotides, they are called **polynucleotides**.
- Each nucleotide consists of a nitrogenous **base**, a pentose **sugar** and a **phosphate** group.

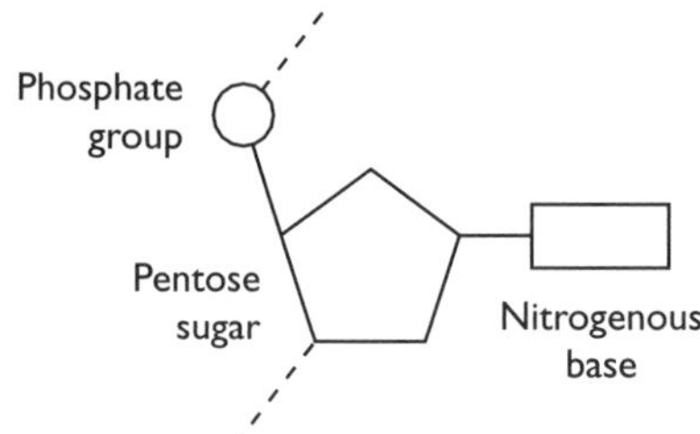

DNA: key facts you must know

- DNA is a double-stranded molecule.
- A molecule of DNA is built from just four types of nucleotide. Each nucleotide differs only in the base it contains. The four bases in DNA nucleotides are **adenine**, **thymine**, **cytosine** and **guanine**, abbreviated to **A**, **T**, **C** and **G**. The pentose sugar found in DNA nucleotides is **deoxyribose**.
- **Adenine** on either strand always bonds with **thymine** on the other strand. **Cytosine** on either strand always bonds with **guanine** on the other strand. This specific pairing is called the **base-pairing rule**.
- Because of the base-pairing rule, the amount of adenine in a DNA molecule is equal to the amount of thymine, and the amount of cytosine is equal to the amount of guanine.
- **Hydrogen bonds** between complementary bases hold the two strands together.

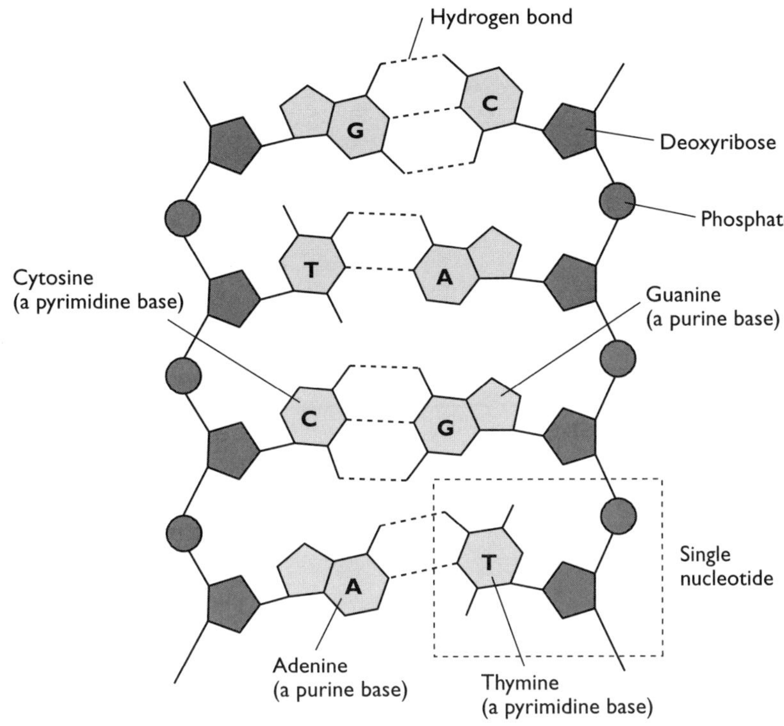

Note: adenine (A) always bonds with thymine (T)
guanine (G) always bonds with cytosine (C)

- The two strands of the DNA molecule are coiled into a helix. The double helix structure of DNA was first proposed by James Watson and Francis Crick in 1953.
- DNA is found in chromosomes in the nucleus of a eukaryotic cell. In prokaryotic cells there is no distinct nucleus and the DNA is free in the cytoplasm.
- Each chromosome contains one molecule of DNA bound to proteins.
- DNA specifies the code for the synthesis of a protein.

RNA: key facts you must know

- There are three types of RNA:
  - **messenger RNA (mRNA)** carries the DNA code for protein synthesis to the ribosomes
  - **transfer RNA (tRNA)** transfers free amino acids to the ribosomes
  - **ribosomal RNA (rRNA)** is a structural component of the ribosomes
- mRNA is a single-stranded linear molecule.
- tRNA is a single-stranded molecule conformed into a cloverleaf shape.
- All three types of RNA differ from DNA in several ways:
  - they are all single-stranded molecules
  - they are all much smaller molecules than DNA
  - the base thymine is replaced by the base **uracil**
  - the pentose sugar in RNA molecules is **ribose** (not deoxyribose)

Tip Note that although tRNA is a single-stranded molecule, there is still some base-pairing. In regions of the molecule where the strand folds back on itself, hydrogen bonds between complementary bases hold the shape of the molecule. Beware of writing that RNA never shows any base-pairing.

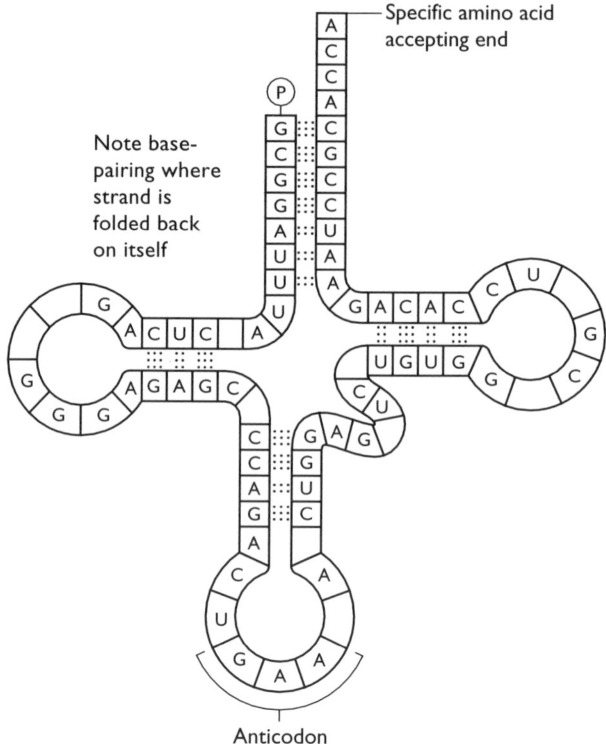

DNA replication

Key facts you must know

- DNA replication occurs during interphase.
- DNA replication is semi-conservative.

T A
A T
T A
C G
G C
A T

The polynucleotide strands of DNA separate…

TA TA
AT AT
TA TA
CG CG
GC GC
AT AT

...each strand acts as a template for the formation of a new molecule of DNA...

...DNA polymerase assembles nucleotides into two new strands according to the base-pairing rule...

TA TA
AT AT
TA TA
CG CG
GC GC
AT AT

...two identical DNA molecules are formed — each contains a strand from the parent DNA and a new complementary strand

Protein synthesis

Key facts you must know

- Proteins are built from chains of amino acids linked by peptide bonds (see Unit 1). This takes place in the **ribosomes**.
- The sequence of amino acids is coded for by the sequence of bases in a gene in a DNA molecule.
- This code is carried from the DNA to the ribosomes by mRNA.
- tRNA carries the free amino acids to the ribosomes where they are assembled into proteins.

The diagram below gives an overview of the stages of protein synthesis.

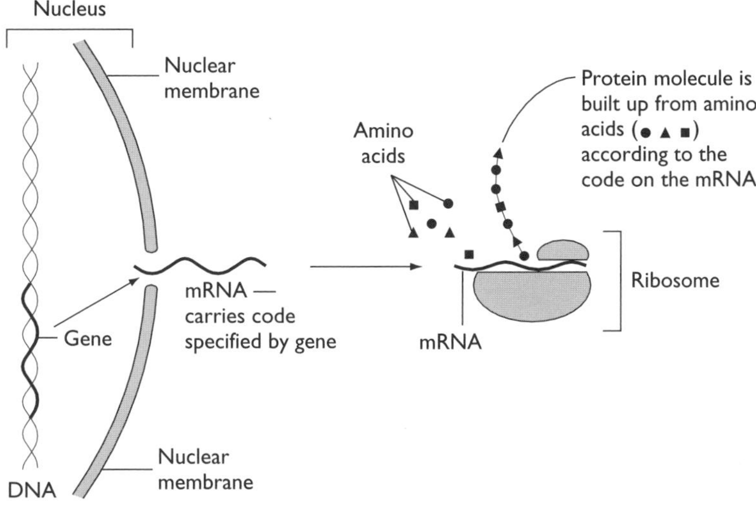

Key concepts you must understand

The DNA code

- The DNA code is a **triplet** code. A sequence of three bases codes for one amino acid.
- The DNA code is a **universal** code. This means that the same triplets of bases code for the same amino acids in all organisms.
- The DNA code is a **degenerate** code. There are 64 possible combinations of the three bases and only 20 amino acids to code for, so some amino acids have more than one code and some triplets do not code for amino acids but carry other information such as a signal to 'stop' because the sequence ends here.

First position	Second position: T	C	A	G	Third position
T	PHE	SER	TYR	CYS	T
	PHE	SER	TYR	CYS	C
	PHE	SER	stop	stop	A
	PHE	SER	stop	TRP	G
C	LEU	PRO	HIS	ARG	T
	LEU	PRO	HIS	ARG	C
	LEU	PRO	GLN	ARG	A
	LEU	PRO	GLN	ARG	G
A	ILE	THR	ASN	SER	T
	ILE	THR	ASN	SER	C
	ILE	THR	LYS	ARG	A
	MET	THR	LYS	ARG	G
G	VAL	ALA	ASP	GLY	T
	VAL	ALA	ASP	GLY	C
	VAL	ALA	GLU	GLY	A
	VAL	ALA	GLU	GLY	G

The DNA code for amino acids

- DNA contains some regions that do not code for anything at all. These are called **non-coding** DNA.

Transcription

The DNA triplet code can be **transcribed** (written in another form) into a triplet mRNA code. Each mRNA triplet is called a **codon** and the bases it contains are complementary to those in a DNA triplet. The main stages in transcription are:

- the section of DNA that is the gene coding for the particular protein unwinds
- RNA polymerase assembles an mRNA strand from free RNA nucleotides according to the base-pairing rule, but uracil is used in the RNA molecule instead of thymine
- any non-coding regions of the mRNA molecule (transcribed from non-coding DNA) are now 'cut out' by enzymes

- the 'finished' mRNA molecule leaves the nucleus through a pore in the nuclear envelope

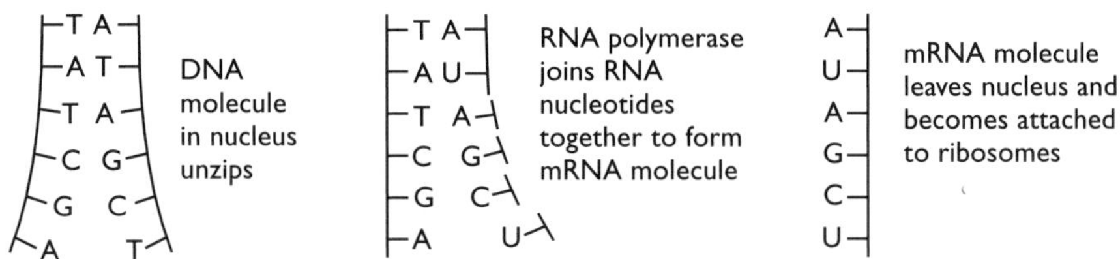

Translation

Translation occurs in the ribosomes. The mRNA molecule feeds through the ribosome and its code is 'translated' into a chain of amino acids.

As the mRNA molecule feeds through the ribosome the following events take place:

- the first two codons on the mRNA molecule are positioned inside the ribosome
- tRNA molecules with complementary **anticodons** and carrying specific amino acids bind with the first two mRNA codons and so carry their amino acids into position
- a peptide bond forms between these two amino acids
- the mRNA moves along by one codon
- the third mRNA codon is now in the ribosome, and tRNA with a complementary anticodon binds to it, bringing its amino acid into position
- a peptide bond forms between the second and third amino acids
- the mRNA moves along by one codon
- the fourth mRNA codon is now in the ribosome...and so on until the last codon (**stop codon**) is in position and translation ceases

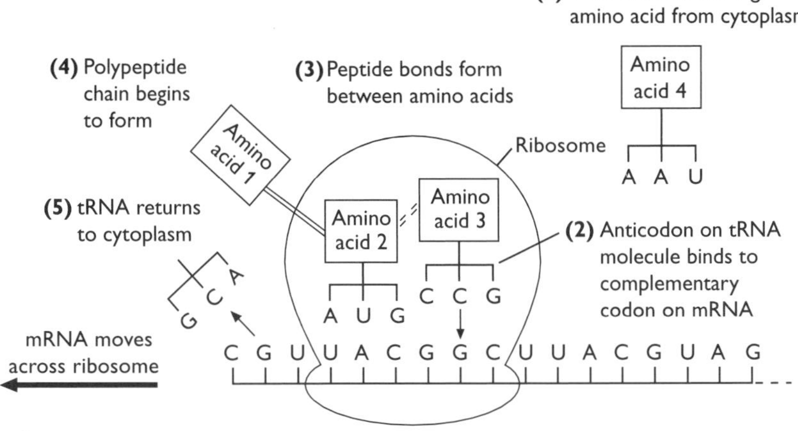

Because DNA codes for all the enzymes synthesised, it controls indirectly all the reactions occurring in cells. Some genes are only active in certain cells and so the particular proteins coded for by those genes are only manufactured in those cells.

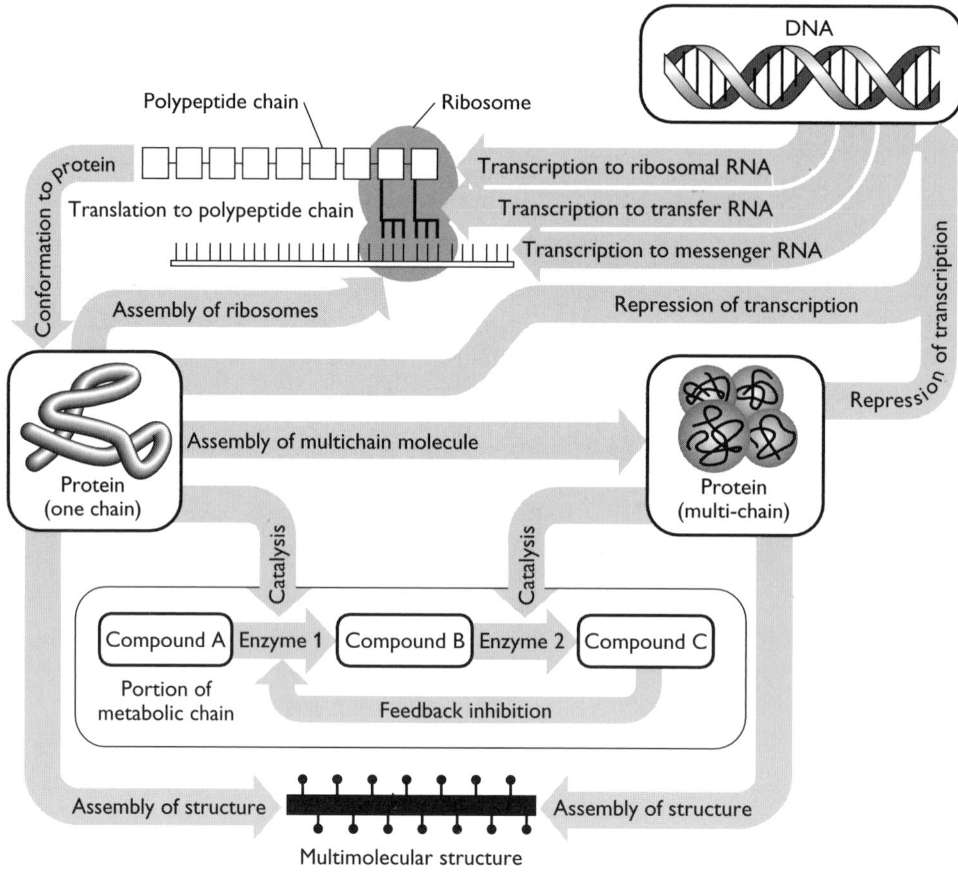

How DNA controls metabolic pathways

What the examiners will expect you to be able to do

- Recall any of the key facts.
- Explain any of the key concepts.
- Identify components of a DNA molecule from a drawing.
- Identify missing bases in a drawing of DNA (use the base-pairing rule — A pairs with T and C pairs with G).
- Calculate percentages of each base in a DNA molecule, given the percentage of just one base.

Tip Remember, because of the base-pairing rule, A = T and C = G *and* A + T + C + G = 100%.
So, if A = 26%,
T is also 26%
A + T = 52%
C + G = 100% – 52% = 48%
C = G, so the value of each is 48% ÷ 2 = 24%

- Describe the sequence of the mRNA strand formed by transcription of a given DNA sequence. (Remember that U is used instead of T in RNA and apply the base-pairing rule.)

Links You will almost certainly have to apply your understanding of the structure of DNA to areas such as meiosis, genetic variation, mutations and natural selection. In plants, protein synthesis is related to photosynthesis, synthesis of amino acids and mineral nutrition.

Genetic engineering

This section looks at the ways in which the genotype of an organism can be modified by the introduction of genes from a different organism and how scientists can be sure that the appropriate genes have been transferred. It also considers whether such practices are ethical.

Key facts you must know

- A section of DNA that codes for a particular polypeptide (or protein) is a **gene**.
- The total complement of genes in an organism is called the **genome**.
- Biotechnologists can show the presence of a gene in a sample of DNA by using a gene-specific DNA probe (gene probe).
- Genes can be 'cut' out of a DNA molecule using **restriction endonucleases**.
- Genes can be inserted ('tied') into another DNA molecule using a **ligase**.

Tip To help you get the names the right way round, remember that *ligation* means tying — think of the *ligature* used in tying back together a surgical wound.

- Genes can be made starting from a molecule of RNA, using an enzyme called **reverse transcriptase**, and then inserted into a molecule of DNA.
- DNA that has had new genes (sections of DNA) added to it is called **recombinant DNA**.
- Genes are transferred into other cells using **vectors**. These are usually either **plasmids** (small pieces of circular DNA found in bacteria) or viruses.

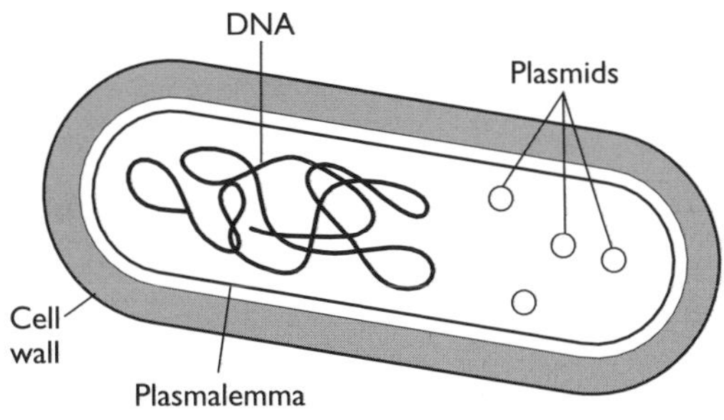

Tip A vector is a means of transfer. The female *Anopheles* mosquito is the vector for the malarial parasite and houseflies are vectors of disease-causing microorganisms. The gene must be inserted into the vector and then the vector carries the gene into the desired cell.

Biotechnologists need to check whether cells have actually taken up plasmids. They do this by seeing if they are resistant to a certain antibiotic. The resistance gene is carried on the same plasmid, so any microorganisms that are resistant must have taken up the plasmid.

An organism that has had DNA from a different organism added is called a **transgenic** organism. By creating appropriate recombinant DNA and inserting it into a microorganism, a transgenic organism can be created that will produce a useful substance (such as human growth hormone or human insulin).

Many people are concerned about the new gene technology and see potential problems such as:

- when a biotechnology company 'creates' a new gene — whose gene is it?
- the technology may accidentally create harmful genes or transfer harmful genes into bacteria used to produce a product for humans; the harmful product of these genes might find its way into humans
- biotechnologists are tampering with God's creation
- genetically modified crop plants are 'not natural' and the genes from these plants might be transferred into other, related, wild plants

Key concepts you must understand

When biotechnologists produce transgenic microorganisms to manufacture a certain product, they must first identify the gene (DNA sequence that codes for the desired product) in the 'donor' cells and remove the gene from these cells. Alternatively, they could create the gene from an appropriate mRNA molecule using reverse transcriptase. They must then transfer the gene to the microorganism using a vector and culture these transgenic microorganisms to give large numbers, so that significant amounts of the product can be synthesised.

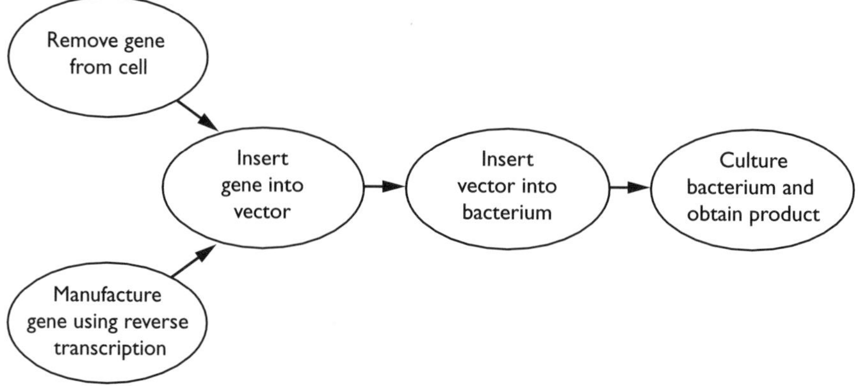

Identifying the gene

To check that a particular gene is present in the donor cells, biotechnologists create a DNA probe (sometimes also called a gene probe). This is a section of single-stranded DNA with a base sequence complementary to that of the gene. The probe is usually made radioactive or fluorescent so that it can be detected.

- The DNA in the donor cells is extracted, split into single strands and mixed with the DNA probe.
- The DNA probe binds with sections of DNA with a complementary base sequence on the gene under investigation.
- Any excess probe is washed off and the remaining DNA is checked for radioactivity (or fluorescence). If it is radioactive (or fluorescent), the probe must have bound to some complementary DNA. The gene must be present.

Removing the gene from the donor cell

The donor cells are incubated with restriction endonuclease enzymes. These enzymes cut the DNA at specific base sequences. By selecting the restriction enzymes carefully, a section of DNA containing the gene can be isolated.

Some restriction enzymes do not make a 'clean cut' across the two strands of the DNA, but make a staggered cut, leaving unpaired bases. These staggered ends are often called '**sticky ends**'.

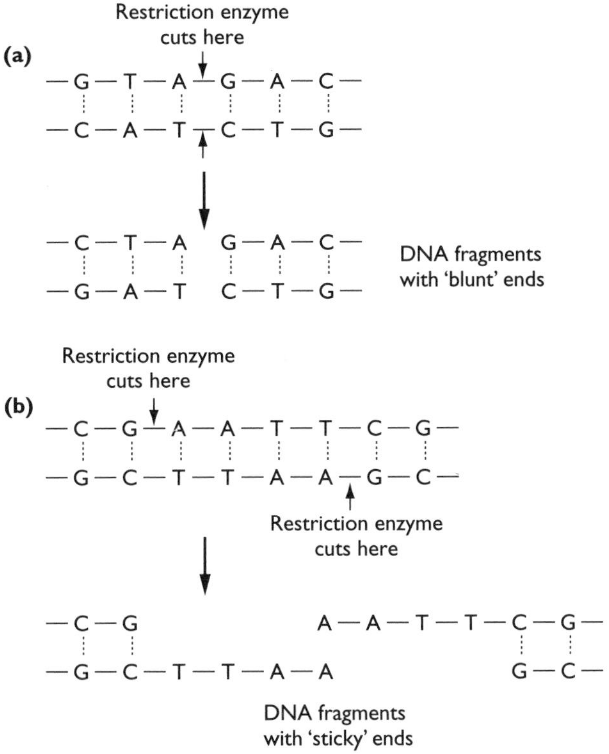

(a)

Restriction enzyme cuts here

—G—T—A—G—A—C—
—C—A—T—C—T—G—

—C—T—A G—A—C—
—G—A—T C—T—G—

DNA fragments with 'blunt' ends

(b)

Restriction enzyme cuts here

—C—G—A—A—T—T—C—G—
—G—C—T—T—A—A—G—C—

Restriction enzyme cuts here

—C—G A—A—T—T—C—G—
—G—C—T—T—A—A G—C—

DNA fragments with 'sticky' ends

Creating the gene from mRNA

- The mRNA molecule coding for the protein is incubated with reverse transcriptase and the necessary free nucleotides.
- Reverse transcriptase creates a single strand of complementary DNA (cDNA).
- The mRNA is 'washed' out.
- The single-stranded DNA is incubated with DNA polymerase and free DNA nucleotides.
- DNA polymerase creates a complementary strand of DNA which bonds with the strand created by reverse transcriptase. (Check the section on DNA replication for further detail.) This double-stranded DNA version of the gene can now be transferred to another cell.

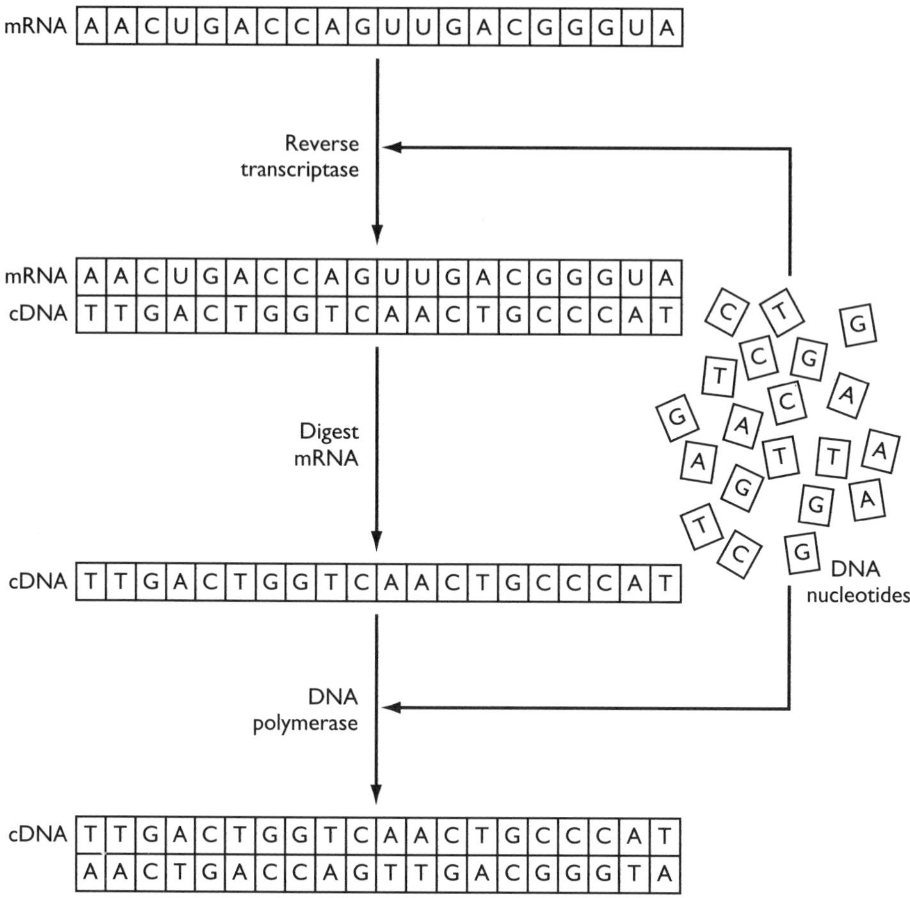

Tip Reverse transcriptase is a very logical name for the enzyme. Think of what happens during transcription — a section of DNA is 'transcribed' to make a mRNA molecule. Throw it into reverse (reverse transcription) and mRNA makes a short, single strand of DNA.

Transferring the gene

Genes are most commonly transferred using plasmids. The diagram below shows the main stages in the process.

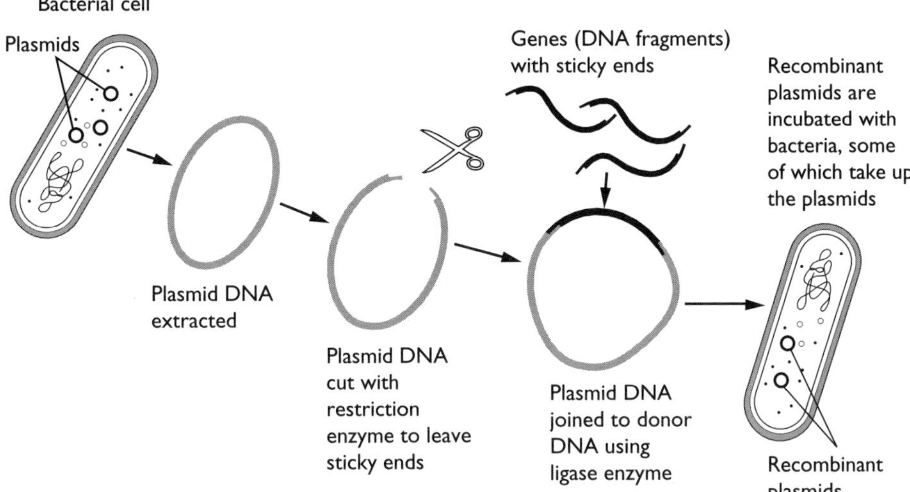

Tip It all sounds very straightforward — snip the gene out with molecular scissors or create the gene with a biochemistry set, glue it into a plasmid and get the bacteria to 'swallow up' the plasmids. However, you must realise that there is only a very small percentage success rate. For example, when the bacteria are incubated with the plasmids, as few as 1 bacterium in 100 000 might actually take up the plasmid! So how do we know that *any* of them have?

Checking that the bacteria have taken up the plasmid

There are a number of ways that this can be done, but it often relies on antibiotic resistance. The procedure is as follows:

- transfer to the plasmids not only the desired gene, but also a gene that gives resistance to a particular antibiotic
- incubate the bacteria with the plasmids
- then culture the bacteria on a medium that contains the antibiotic

Only those bacteria that are resistant to the antibiotic can survive. To be resistant, they must have taken up the plasmid so they must *also* have the desired gene.

Culturing the transgenic microorganisms

Once the transgenic bacteria have been identified, they are cultured in a liquid medium, initially on a relatively small scale. As the bacteria reproduce, so does the plasmid containing the new gene. The new gene is copied into all the bacteria — we say that the gene has been **cloned**. Once the bacteria have multiplied, an **inoculum** from this culture is transferred to a much larger fermenter, where the bacteria multiply and produce the desired substance (e.g. human insulin or human growth hormone). Downstream processing then isolates and purifies the product.

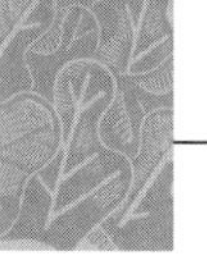

What the examiners will expect you to be able to do

- Recall any of the key facts.
- Explain any of the key concepts.
- Complete flow charts showing the different stages of genetic manipulation.
- Interpret information given about a new example.
- Explain why the product from a transgenic microorganism is identical to that from the original cell.
- Comment, from data given, on possible advantages and disadvantages of a particular process.

Links Genetic engineering is making advances daily and genes are being transferred into many organisms to try to combat genetic disorders. Cystic fibrosis is just one example of gene therapy, where genes are introduced into human cells to try to combat such a disorder. Cells from the pituitary gland in mice have been genetically engineered to produce insulin and reintroduced into diabetic mice to control their diabetes. Plants are being genetically engineered to make them more able to survive in particular environments. You may be asked about genetic engineering in other modules where such topics are covered. For example, what would be the benefit of engineering other crop plants to fix nitrogen as legumes can?

Using biotechnology in forensic science

This section looks at the ways in which some aspects of biotechnology can be used for identification of suspects. Blood grouping is a well-known technique which can provide evidence to eliminate a suspect, but which cannot, on its own, prove guilt. The more modern technique of genetic fingerprinting is also considered, as well as the polymerase chain reaction (PCR) which can be used to provide enough DNA for analysis from a tiny sample.

Immunology and blood grouping

Key facts you must know

- Cells have 'markers' on their surface (often glycoproteins) called **antigens**.
- **Antibodies** are proteins (of a type called immunoglobulins) which can bind with antigens. Each antibody recognises and binds with just one antigen.

- Antibodies are produced by **plasma cells** which are formed by the multiplication of **B lymphocytes**.

Each B lymphocyte has the potential to produce a different antibody. When disease-causing bacteria or viruses enter our body, an **immune response** results. Some B lymphocytes recognise the antigens on the surface of the microorganisms. These B lymphocytes multiply and form millions of larger **plasma cells**. The plasma cells manufacture and release specific antibodies which can bind with the antigens on the microorganisms.

Some of the original B lymphocytes do not form plasma cells but form **memory cells**. These cells remain in the bloodstream and form the basis of our **immunity** to that particular disease. If microorganisms of the same type enter our body again, the memory cells recognise their antigens, multiply and form plasma cells. This happens much quicker than the initial response, so that more antibodies are produced before the infecting microorganism has time to multiply and cause disease.

The antigens on the surface of red blood cells allow us to place people in different blood groups. There are 14 different systems of genetically determined blood groups involving over 100 antigens. You need to know about the **ABO system** only.

In this system there are just four possible blood groups, **A**, **B**, **AB** and **O**. These are determined by the presence or absence of just two antigens on the red blood cells — the **A antigen** and the **B antigen**.

Besides the antigen on the red blood cells, there are also antibodies present in the blood plasma. These antibodies cause **agglutination** (clumping) of the red cells when they bind with the corresponding antigen. The antibodies are **a** (causes red cells with antigen **A** to agglutinate) and **b** (causes red cells with antigen **B** to agglutinate). Agglutination could be fatal since it could lead to a blockage of an artery, such as one of the coronary arteries.

Blood group	Antigen present (on red blood cells)	Antibody present (in blood plasma)
A	A	b
B	B	a
AB	A + B	Neither
O	Neither	a + b

Tip These antibodies are present *all the time* in our plasma. They are *not* formed as part of the immune response by B lymphocytes in the way other antibodies are formed.

Key concepts you must understand

- Antibodies can only bind with one specific antigen because of the shapes of the two molecules.

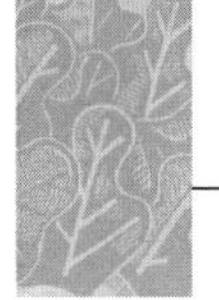

- Parts of the molecules must have complementary shapes to allow them to bind.

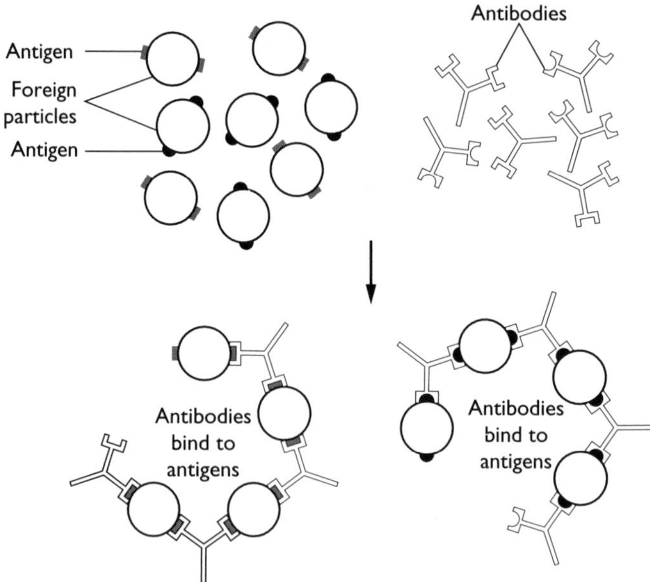

The formation of plasma cells from B lymphocytes is called **clonal selection**. This is because the antigens on the surface of invading microorganisms are recognised by only the B lymphocytes which could produce antibodies against them. Only these B lymphocytes are **selected** or activated. They then divide many times by mitosis, forming a **clone** of the original cell.

The body does not normally make antibodies against its own antigens because these are recognised as **self**. Antigens not in this 'set' are **non-self** and stimulate an immune response.

A person's blood group can be identified by mixing a sample of their blood with an antibody preparation. The following occur due to antigen/antibody reaction:

Blood group	Reaction with antibody a	Reaction with antibody b
A	**Agglutination**	No reaction
B	No reaction	**Agglutination**
AB	**Agglutination**	**Agglutination**
O	No reaction	No reaction

Knowing a suspect's blood group can eliminate them from a criminal investigation but cannot alone prove guilt. Millions of people share the same blood group.

When blood is transfused, the main risk of agglutination comes from the antigens on the red blood cells from the blood donor reacting with the antibodies in the plasma of the recipient. Unsafe and safe transfusions are shown in the following table.

Blood group of donor (antigen in brackets)	Blood group of recipient (antibodies in brackets) A (b)	B (a)	AB (none)	O (a + b)
A (A)	Safe	Unsafe	Safe	Unsafe
B (B)	Unsafe	Safe	Safe	Unsafe
AB (A + B)	Unsafe	Unsafe	Safe	Unsafe
O (none)	Safe	Safe	Safe	Safe

Notice that wherever there is any correspondence between the donor antigen and the recipient antibody, the transfusion is unsafe because agglutination would result.

Blood group O is the **universal donor**, while blood group AB is the **universal recipient**.

Genetic fingerprinting

Key facts you must know

Unlike blood groups, a 'genetic fingerprint' is unique (identical twins who have identical DNA are the exception). Because of this, a genetic fingerprint can indicate guilt as well as innocence. **Non-coding** DNA provides the basis of a genetic fingerprint.

The main steps in genetic fingerprinting are listed below:

- a sample of the DNA is obtained (usually from blood in criminal investigations)
- if there is insufficient DNA, more is made using the **polymerase chain reaction (PCR)**
- the DNA is cut into sections using a restriction endonuclease
- the sections of DNA are separated using **electrophoresis**
- the separated DNA is transferred to a membrane
- radioactive DNA probes are applied to the membrane
- the regions where the DNA probe binds are identified using X-ray film
- the resulting pattern (which resembles a complicated bar code) is a genetic fingerprint

Key concepts you must understand

Many proteins are identical in all individuals. This means that their amino acid sequence is identical and so must be the DNA sequence that codes for them. Much of the coding DNA is the same in all individuals. Non-coding DNA varies from one person to the next and forms the basis of a genetic fingerprint.

A restriction enzyme is used to cut the DNA close to, but not within, non-coding sections. As a result, many coding sequences are disrupted, but non-coding DNA sequences are left intact.

Because the lengths of the non-coding sequences vary, the size of the DNA fragments produced will vary. These can be separated by gel electrophoresis.

Electrophoresis separates fragments of DNA partly by the charge on the molecule but mainly by the physical size of the fragment. Molecular mass depends on size and so can be calculated from distance moved.

Once separation is complete, the fragments are carefully transferred to a membrane before having DNA probes applied. These are carefully chosen to bind with sequences found within the non-coding sections. After washing the probe out, the regions where the probes have bound are displayed using X-ray film that becomes 'fogged' when exposed to radioactivity. The resulting pattern is the DNA fingerprint.

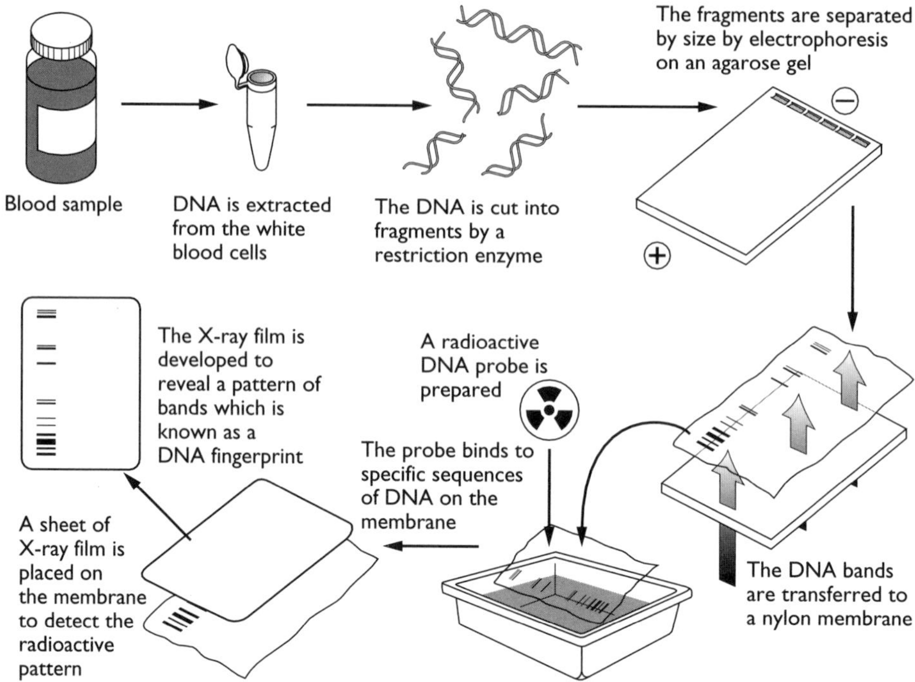

The polymerase chain reaction (PCR)

Key facts you must know

- The polymerase chain reaction is an automated method for increasing the amount of DNA available, without the need to clone it in transgenic organisms.
- The strands of DNA are separated by heating and then a complementary strand is made for each by using DNA polymerase and free nucleotides.
- The DNA is replicated using the same principles as semi-conservative replication in the cell.
- The cycle of separation and replication is repeated many times to build up many copies of the original DNA.

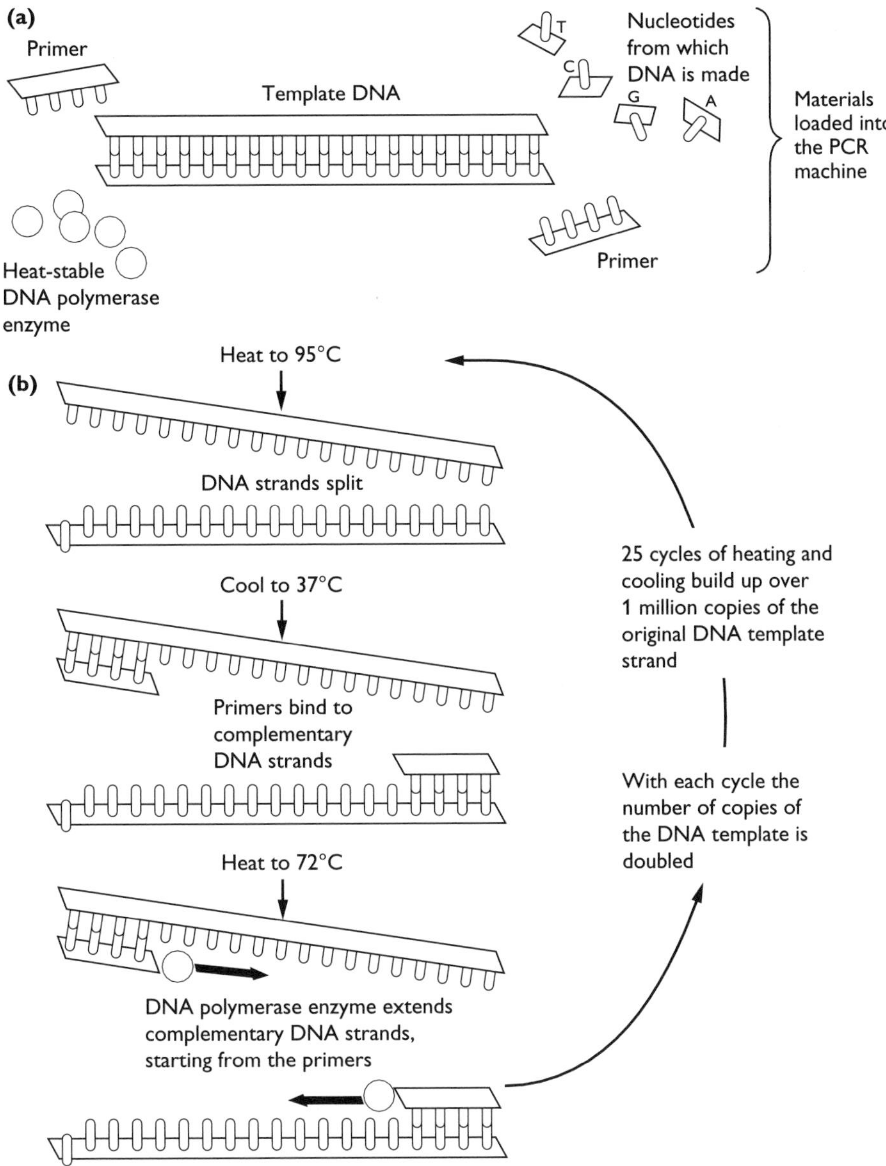

Using a thermostable enzyme allows the process to be continuous. High temperatures do not denature it, so there is no need to add new enzyme after each cycle.

Theoretically, each cycle doubles the number of DNA molecules available for analysis. The total number of DNA molecules produced is given by the formula:

$$T = N \times 2^{C}$$

where T is the total number of DNA molecules produced, N is the number of DNA molecules at the start and C is the number of cycles. After 25 cycles, starting with just

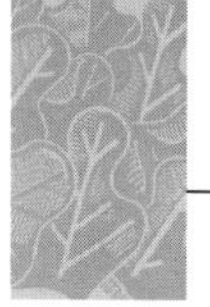

one molecule of DNA, there should be $1 \times 2^{25} = 33\,554\,432$ molecules of DNA! In practice, no reaction ever proceeds with 100% efficiency and so there is nowhere near this number of molecules formed. Still, 25 cycles yield over 1 million copies of each molecule of DNA.

What the examiners will expect you to be able to do

- Recall any of the key facts.
- Explain any of the key concepts.
- Given information about the function of a particular antigen, deduce the effect of causing the body to make antibodies against it and therefore block its function.
- Explain why a second immune response is quicker and stronger than the first.
- Explain why a particular blood transfusion is safe or unsafe.
- Deduce a person's blood group from the reaction with antibodies.
- Explain why non-coding DNA is the basis of genetic fingerprinting.
- From information given, identify fragments of DNA on diagrams showing the results of electrophoresis.
- Use the PCR formula to calculate the theoretical number of DNA molecules from a given starting point.
- Explain the benefits of using a thermostable DNA polymerase in the PCR.

Links Although largely self-contained, there are some links between this section and others. For example, the pattern of inheritance of blood groups, not covered in this section, may be covered in Module 5.

Crop production: getting the best yields

This section looks at the adaptations of cereal crops to specific environments. It also considers the ways in which the environment can be controlled to maximise crop yield. This includes providing optimum conditions for photosynthesis in commercial greenhouses, the use of fertilisers to increase yields as well as methods of pest control to prevent reduction in yield. Integrated crop management uses a range of techniques to obtain the best yield.

Adaptations of cereals

Key facts you must know

Cereals are important crop plants, belonging to the grass family, which form a major component of the diet of millions of people. They have been selectively bred for increased grain yield. Cereal grains are an important part of the diet because they contain:

- large amounts of starch and therefore yield large amounts of energy per gram
- relatively large amounts of protein (9–14%)
- significant amounts of the essential amino acids in the protein
- significant amounts of the B vitamins
- little fat and virtually no sugar

Rice

Different strains of rice are now grown in many countries in different ways. Traditionally, however, it was grown in southeast Asia in 'paddy fields', with much of the plant under water.

Rice is specifically adapted to its environment in a number of ways.

- The growing plant elongates by up to 10 cm per day. This ensures that, as water levels rise around the plant, although much of the plant becomes submerged, the upper shoot (stem, leaves and flower) remain out of the water.
- Much of the stem and root tissue is **aerenchyma**, a specialised tissue which contains many air spaces. This allows easy diffusion of oxygen and carbon dioxide through the plant. Oxygen cannot easily be obtained by the submerged parts of the plant and so must pass through the plants from those regions above water. The aerenchyma, because of its structure, retains much of the normal strength of a normal stem. Also, the rapid elongation is possible in part due to the aerenchyma. Fewer cells need be produced.

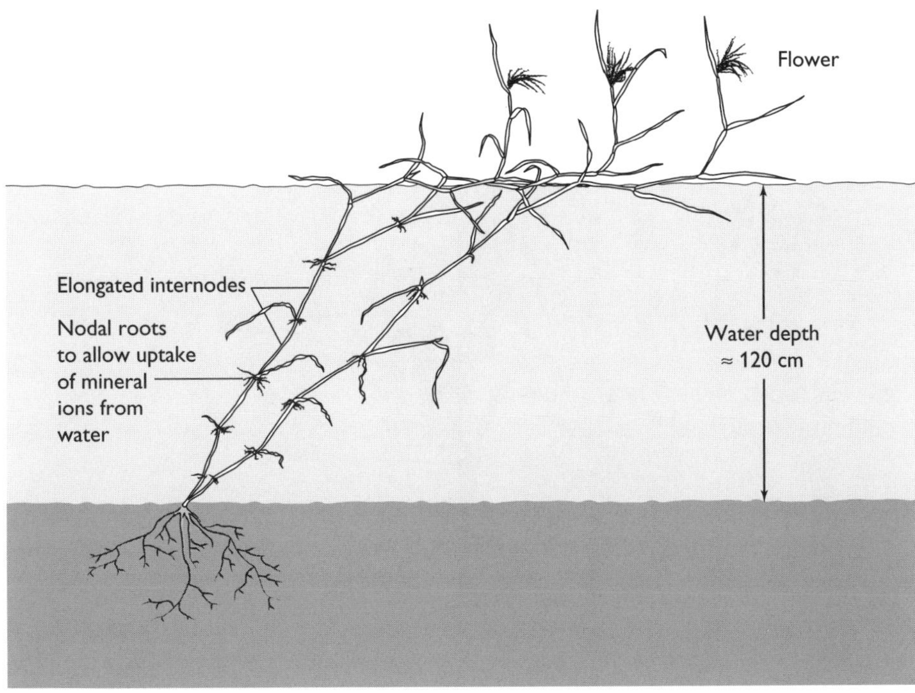

- Rice is tolerant to high levels of ethanol. Sometimes, the entire plant is submerged by flood water for several days. Under these conditions, the cells will respire anaerobically. Ethanol tolerance allows the rice plant to survive until the water levels fall.
- Additional roots develop from submerged stems. These absorb mineral ions from the surrounding water.

Maize

Maize is more commonly known as corn or sweetcorn. The familiar 'corn on the cob' is the product of the maize plant.

Maize is essentially a tropical plant. It is adapted to grow efficiently in hot, sunny conditions where the concentration of carbon dioxide in the air is the main factor limiting the rate of photosynthesis and, therefore, productivity.

Maize has a specialised method of photosynthesis (called C4 photosynthesis) which is more efficient than the normal process at low carbon dioxide concentrations and high temperatures. Therefore in the tropical and subtropical countries where it is mainly cultivated, maize can give high crop yields.

Sorghum

Sorghum is a cultivated grass found mainly in Africa. Its grains are used for making a paste which can be baked to form a kind of bread. Sorghum is a xerophyte, i.e. it has several adaptations that enable it to grow in hot, dry conditions. These mainly help the plant to obtain as much water as possible or reduce water loss.

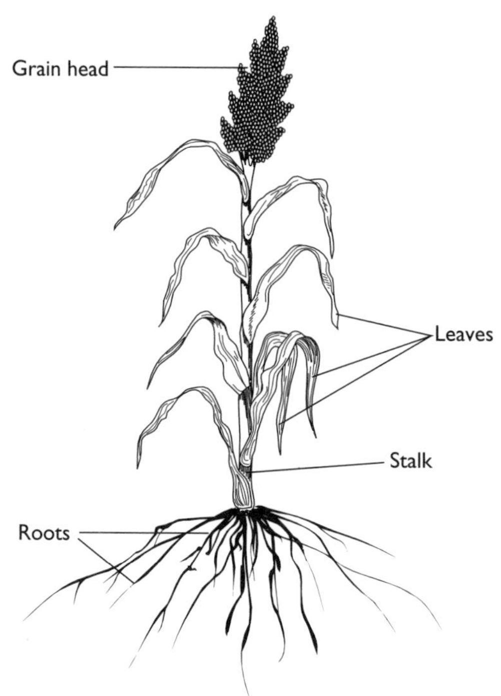

- It has a deep and extensive root system, which allows the plant to absorb as much water as possible.
- It has a reduced number of stomata, which are mostly sunken below the lower epidermis of the leaf. Both these features help to reduce water loss by transpiration.
- The leaves have thin-walled cells in the lower surfaces which allow an initial rapid loss of water. The leaves then curl up to form a tube, with the lower surfaces on the inside of this tube. Inside the tube a layer of moist air forms which restricts further loss of water by reducing the diffusion gradient to virtually zero.

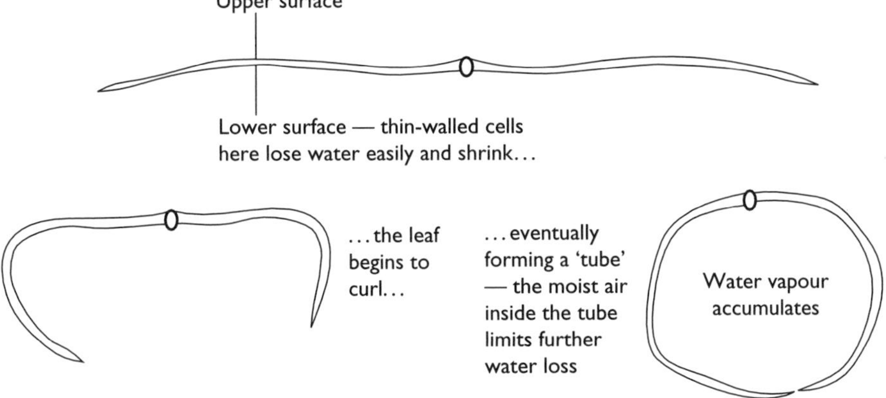

Like maize, sorghum uses C4 photosynthesis.

Enhancing productivity by controlling the environment

The productivity of crop plants depends on how efficiently they can synthesise the chemicals needed for growth. This, in turn, depends on how efficiently they can photosynthesise and absorb mineral ions. Commercial growers enhance the conditions necessary for photosynthesis in commercial glasshouses (large greenhouses) and use fertilisers to replace mineral ions lost by harvesting crops.

Key facts you must know

Photosynthesis produces the carbohydrates that are the basis of all other nutrient production in plants. Photosynthesis depends on:

- a supply of carbon dioxide (a raw material)
- a supply of water (a raw material)
- light energy (to 'drive' the process)
- chlorophyll (to absorb the light energy)

- a suitable temperature (many of the reactions of photosynthesis are controlled by enzymes which are affected by temperature)

The rate of photosynthesis is, therefore, influenced by all of these factors.

Key concepts you must understand

Growing crops in large greenhouses (glasshouses) allows the environment to be controlled to enhance photosynthesis and so increase productivity.

The greenhouse effect happens in greenhouses as well as in the Earth's atmosphere! Short-wave radiation entering becomes longer-wave radiation as it strikes a surface in the greenhouse. This cannot escape as easily, so the greenhouse warms up.

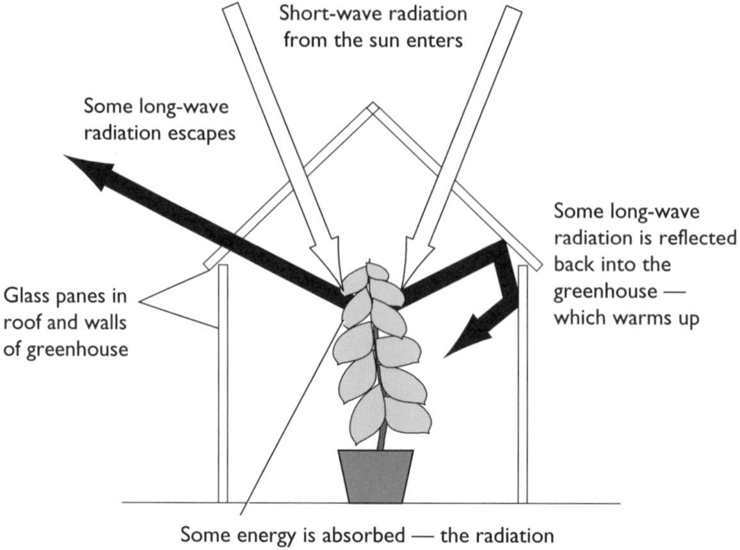

Increasing the temperature in a greenhouse increases the rate of photosynthesis because it increases the rate of enzyme–substrate complex formation between the enzymes controlling photosynthesis and their substrates.

Increasing the concentration of carbon dioxide will also increase the rate of enzyme–substrate complex formation as carbon dioxide is a key substrate. The concentration of carbon dioxide can be increased by burning fuel in the greenhouse. This has the added benefit of increasing the temperature.

Photosynthesis is influenced by light intensity, temperature and carbon dioxide concentration. If any of these is in short supply it will restrict or *limit* the rate of photosynthesis. This is called the **law of limiting factors**.

Tip Think of a group of cyclists — to stay as a group, they must cycle at the speed of the slowest.

If a factor limiting photosynthesis is increased, the rate of photosynthesis increases. If the factor is non-limiting (i.e. something else is limiting), then increasing the factor will have no effect.

The graph below shows the effect of increasing light intensity on the rate of photosynthesis.

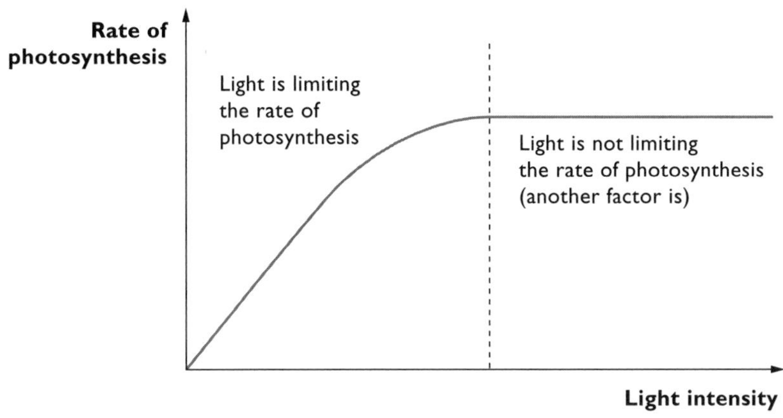

Where light is limiting, increasing its intensity increases the rate of photosynthesis. As light becomes increasingly abundant, something else limits the process. The light is now non-limiting.

Now look at the graph below, which shows the effect of light intensity on the rate of photosynthesis at different carbon dioxide concentrations.

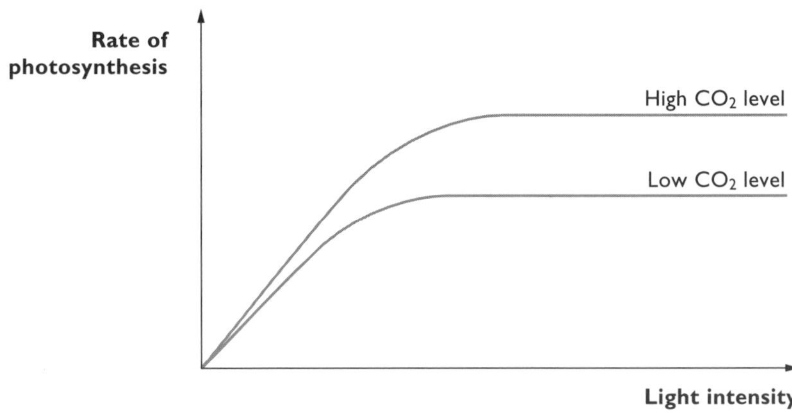

Both lines have the same basic shape, and light eventually becomes non-limiting in both. The point at which this happens is different because when more carbon dioxide is available, increasing the light intensity allows an even faster reaction.

Finally, consider the following graph. It shows the same effects as the previous graph,

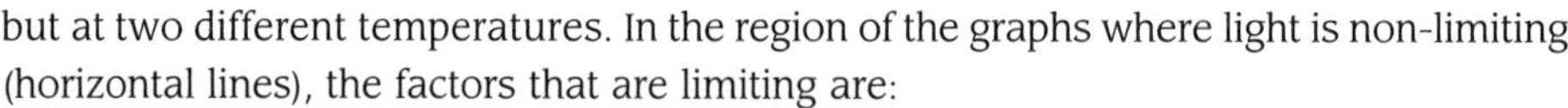

but at two different temperatures. In the region of the graphs where light is non-limiting (horizontal lines), the factors that are limiting are:

- **A** — both temperature and carbon dioxide; increasing either produces an increase in the rate of photosynthesis to level **B** or **C**
- **B** — temperature (the factor that hasn't been increased from **A**); increasing the temperature increases the rate to level **D**
- **C** — carbon dioxide (the factor that hasn't been increased from **A**); increasing the carbon dioxide concentration increases the rate to level **D**

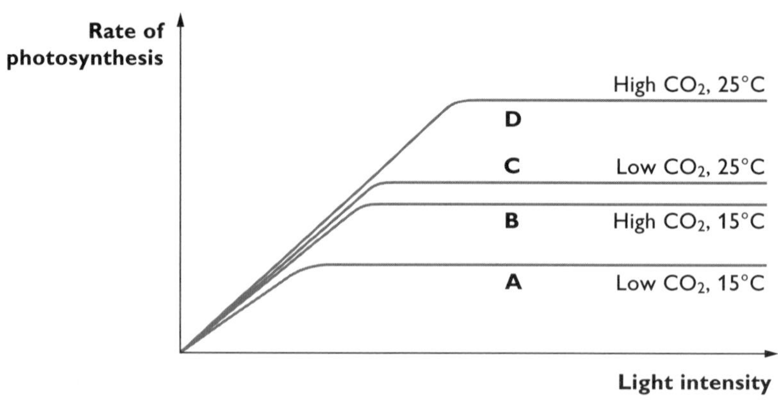

Increasing the temperature increases the rate of photosynthesis until it becomes limiting. After a certain point, increasing the temperature decreases the rate, as the enzymes controlling the reactions start to denature.

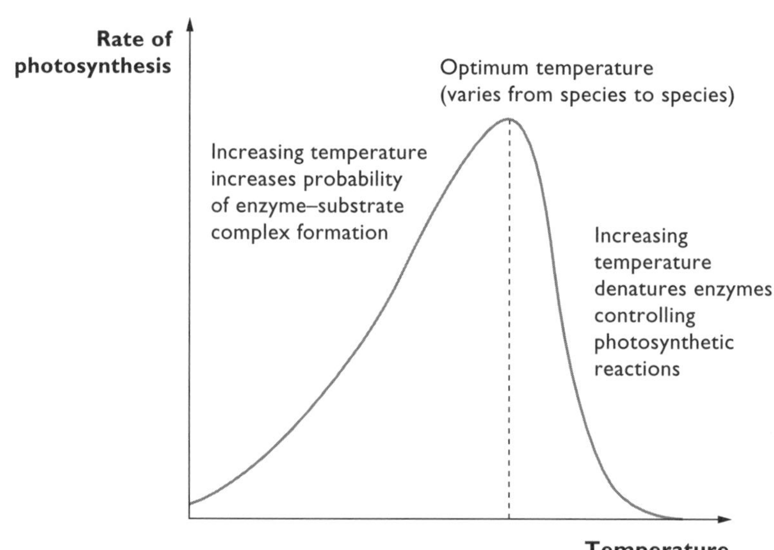

Using fertilisers

Key facts you must know

Fertilisers are used to enrich the soil with mineral ions such as nitrate (NO_3^-), phosphate (PO_4^{3-}) and potassium (K^+). Nitrate is important in the synthesis of amino acids (and therefore proteins), ATP and DNA. Phosphate is important in the synthesis of ATP, DNA, RNA and phospholipids. Potassium activates over 40 enzymes in plants.

When crops are harvested, many of the mineral ions that they absorbed during growth are harvested with them. If this is repeated year after year it leaves the soil 'nutrient-poor'. Fertilisers can replace the ions removed by harvesting.

Farmers use organic and inorganic fertilisers. Organic fertilisers are materials produced directly from animals and plants. They include materials like farmyard manure, dried blood, sewage sludge and poultry manure.

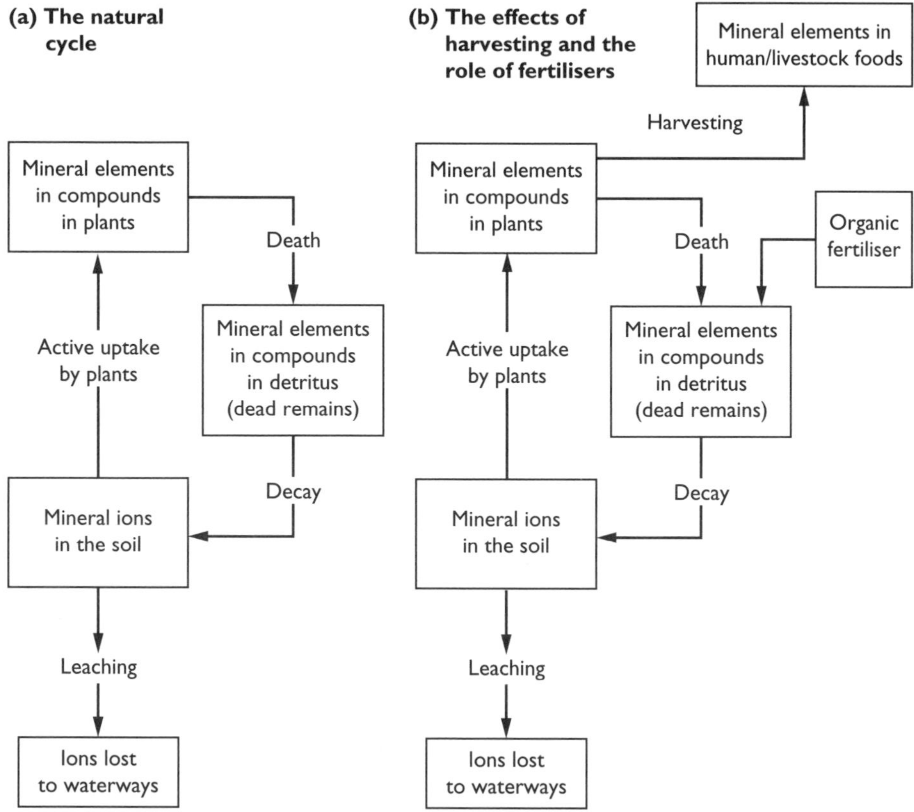

Inorganic fertilisers contain soluble mineral ions which are easily washed out of the soil (**leached**) by rain. This can pollute waterways and lead to **eutrophication**.

Key concepts you must understand

In the normal cycle of growth, death and decay of plants, mineral ions removed from the soil for plant growth are returned to the soil when the plant dies. This happens when the plant is decomposed by soil microorganisms.

Harvesting crop plants breaks this cycle and the mineral ions are not returned to the soil, which becomes mineral-poor.

The use of fertilisers puts back the mineral ions removed by harvesting. If an organic fertiliser is used, it must be decomposed in the same way as detritus before the mineral ions are released. It is therefore a **slow-release** fertiliser, releasing only small amounts of ions per kilogram. Inorganic fertilisers do not need to be broken down because they are already in the form of mineral ions and are **quick-release** fertilisers yielding large amounts of ions per kilogram.

Because of the rate of release of the ions, the two types of fertiliser need to be applied at different times:

- slow-release organic fertilisers should be applied some time before the main demand from the crop plants to allow time for decay and release of the ions
- quick-release inorganic fertilisers should be applied as the crops approach their peak demand

Organic fertilisers can improve yields in other ways. The dark colour of organic manure absorbs heat better and helps the soil to warm up faster in spring, aiding germination of seeds. The organic material improves the structure of the soil, giving good drainage and aeration, yet still allowing quite good water retention. This means there is always adequate oxygen and water in the soil to allow efficient absorption of mineral ions.

Overuse of either type of fertiliser can have serious consequences, although these are more likely to occur with inorganic fertilisers. Because of their high solubility, inorganic fertilisers are easily leached from (washed out of) the soil. They may enter waterways where they can encourage eutrophication.

The problem arises because algae need just the same mineral ions for growth as do crop plants. When the level of mineral ions in a waterway rises, the following chain of events can occur:

- algae multiply rapidly (increased protein synthesis is possible) and either form a mat over the surface or, in the case of unicellular algae, form an algal bloom
- the increased numbers of algae reduce the transmission of light to lower levels
- plants growing at lower levels cannot photosynthesise effectively and can die
- many of the algae die as the ions are used up
- microorganisms start to decompose the dead algae
- the microorganisms use oxygen (in aerobic respiration) in increasing amounts as they multiply
- the levels of oxygen in the water fall dramatically and many animals suffocate
- as the bacteria release mineral ions from the dead algae, the process might start again

Eutrophication is more likely to occur in hot weather because:
- the mineral ions become even more concentrated in waterways due to increased evaporation of water
- all the processes involved are speeded up (due to increased enzyme activity)

Eutrophication is less likely to occur in moving water because:
- the mineral ions are rapidly diluted
- the water is continually being re-oxygenated

Organic fertilisers are less likely to cause these problems because:
- the organic materials are less soluble and so are not leached easily from soils
- they release the mineral ions slowly over a longer period of time

Controlling pests

Key facts you must understand

Pests are organisms that reduce the productivity of crops. They are not just animals — weeds are also pests.

From the crop growers' point of view, weeds are plants growing in the wrong place. The weeds compete with the crop plants for the available light, water, carbon dioxide and mineral ions. This is called **interspecific competition** because it is competition *between* members of two different species, i.e. the weed and the crop plant.

Tip If you get confused between *inter*- and *intra*specific competition, just remember an *inter*-national match is *between* members of *two different nations*.

Weeds often have higher growth rates than the crops with which they compete. They establish their root and shoot systems quicker and obtain more of the available resources, reducing the availability to the crop plants and so reducing yields.

The effects of pests can depend on the density of the crop planting. Sometimes there is very little effect at low crop densities, but a much bigger reduction in yield at high crop densities.

Some insects are pests. They can reduce the yield of the crop in a number of ways:
- they can feed directly on the organ of the plant that forms the 'crop' (e.g. the carrot fly feeds on the young tap root of the carrot plant; the caterpillars (larvae) of the pea moth feed on the peas maturing inside the pea pod)
- they can reduce the yield by feeding on the leaves; this reduces the leaf area and therefore the capacity of the plant for photosynthesis
- they can feed on and damage the roots, restricting the uptake of mineral ions essential for growth (e.g. the cabbage root fly feeds on cabbage roots, stunting growth)
- they can feed from the phloem and so disrupt the transfer of sugars manufactured in photosynthesis to other organs (aphids reduce crop yields in this way)

- they can spread organisms that cause disease (e.g. the potato aphid can introduce a virus that causes 'leaf-roll'; this reduces the area of leaf exposed to the light and so reduces photosynthesis)

A **pesticide** is a chemical that helps to control the population of a pest. Pesticides can be classified according to the type of organism they control, for example:
- **insecticides** kill insects
- **herbicides** kill plants (they are weedkillers)
- **fungicides** kill fungi
- **molluscicides** kill molluscs (slugs and snails)

Some pesticides have effects on organisms in the environment other than the pests they are used to control. These effects include the following:
- insecticides might kill useful insects as well as the targeted harmful insects
- pesticides might persist in the environment for many years before they are finally broken down (it can take up to 25 years to break down an application of DDT)
- herbicides can remain in the soil for long periods, be taken up by crop plants and so enter humans through the food chain
- some pesticides (such as DDT) accumulate along food chains (**bioaccumulation**)

Sometimes using a chemical pesticide is an ineffective method of pest control because the pests can become resistant to the pesticide. In these circumstances **biological control** methods may be used. This involves introducing a natural parasite or predator of the pest into the area with the aim of reducing the pest population.

Tip Be careful how you describe pesticide resistance in an examination. Some candidates describe it as 'becoming immune' to the pesticide. This is wrong. Immunity results from the exposure of an *individual* to an antigen. This provokes an *immediate* immune reaction and the *individual* becomes immune. Pesticide resistance results from the exposure of a *population* to a pesticide. Those individuals that are resistant have a selective advantage. Natural selection ensures that they survive to reproduce and pass on their 'resistant' genes. More and more of the *population* become resistant *over a period of time*.

Often, farmers use a combination of biological control and chemical control to reduce pest populations. This is called **integrated control**.

Key concepts you must understand

The aim of pest control is to reduce the level of pest populations to the point where they no longer cause serious economic damage to the crops.

When pesticides are applied, they are never 100% effective, for two main reasons:
- the application procedure is never 100% effective — some of the pests do not come into contact with the pesticide or receive only a limited 'dose'
- some individuals of the pest population have some resistance to the pesticide

As a result, some individuals survive, with the resistant types having more chance of survival. So, by natural selection, the numbers resistant to the pesticide increase in the population after each application of the pesticide. Successive applications kill fewer and fewer pests as the proportion of resistant individuals increases. Eventually, nearly all the population is resistant and the pesticide is of limited use.

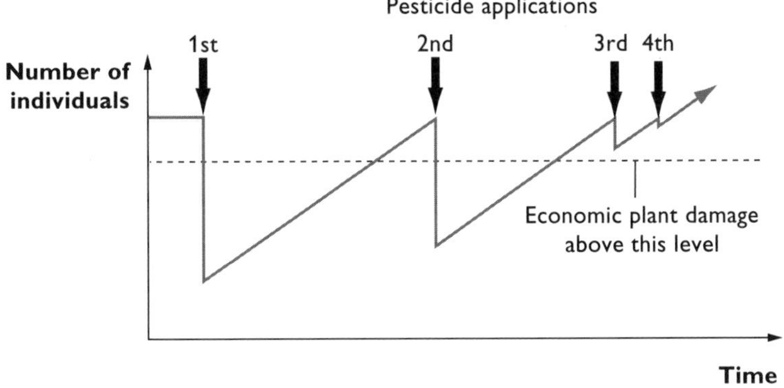

Besides the effect of pesticide resistance, there is another effect known as **pest resurgence**. After pesticide application, the pest population is reduced. However, some pesticides are not very selective and might also kill natural predators of the pest. The pest population recovers to a higher level than before.

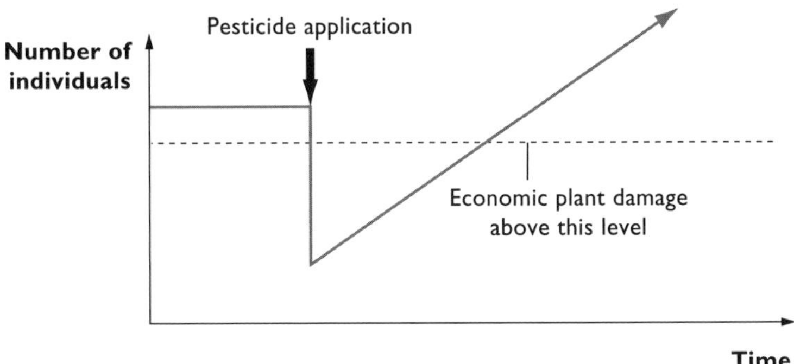

Bioaccumulation of pesticides along a food chain results in very high levels of a pesticide in organisms at the end of the chain, resulting from what seem to be normal applications. A classic example of this is the bioaccumulation of DDT. DDT is an insecticide which persists in the environment and, when taken up by organisms, is stored in body fat. A consumer usually eats many organisms. If each of these is contaminated with DDT, the 'dose' received by the consumer is the total amount of DDT stored in all their bodies. This is then repeated at each link of the food chain.

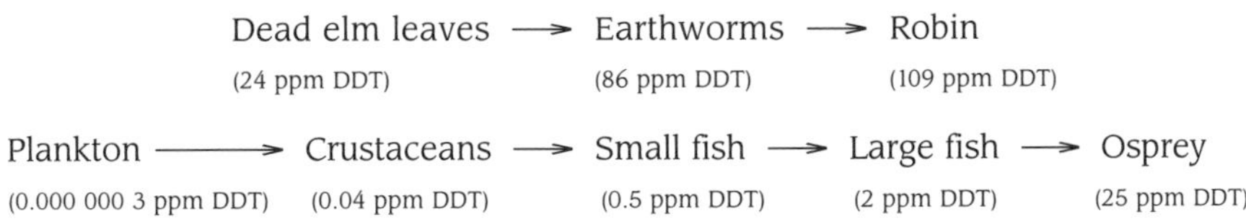

An ideal pesticide should:

- control the pest effectively
- be specific, so that *only* the pest is controlled
- be biodegradable
- *not* accumulate along food chains
- be safe to store and transport
- be easy and safe to apply

Biological control

Biological control methods do not aim to eradicate a pest but rather to reduce the pest numbers to a level at which they do not cause major economic damage.

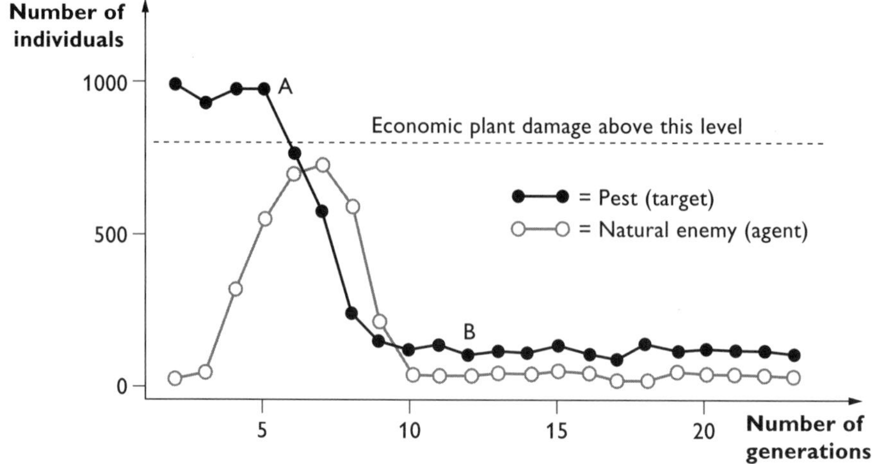

Biological control methods include the following examples:

- introducing a **predator** — for example, ladybirds have been introduced to orange groves to control aphid populations which reduce the yield of oranges
- introducing a **herbivore** — for example, a moth native to South America was introduced to Australia to control the 'prickly pear' cactus, which was taking over vast areas of arable land
- introducing a **parasite** — for example, larvae of the wasp *Encarsia* parasitise whiteflies which can devastate tomato crops in greenhouses
- introducing **sterile males** — this reduces the number of successful matings and so reduces the pest numbers
- using **pheromones** — these animal sex hormones are used to attract the males or females, which are then destroyed. Reproduction is reduced and numbers decline. Male-attracting pheromones are used to control the damson-hop aphid, reducing damage to plum crops.

Biological control has several advantages over the use of pesticides:

- pests do not usually develop resistance to a predator or parasite
- biological control agents are usually much more specific than pesticides; for example, a carefully chosen predator will target only the pest, whereas a

pesticide might target all the animals of a particular group (an insecticide might kill many kinds of insect)

- once a natural predator or parasite has been introduced, no further reintroductions are necessary, whereas pesticides must often be re-applied

At first glance, it seems that biological control systems cannot fail and should always be used. However, there are a number of potential problems.

- Research is necessary to ensure that the proposed control agent will control only the pest population. It might also target other, similar organisms as well as natural predators of the pest in the area. It must be clear too that any newly introduced control agent will actually survive and reproduce in the new conditions.
- Using biological control to reduce the numbers of one specific pest may allow another pest to fill its ecological niche. Occasionally, this can make matters worse.
- Biological control is not an appropriate method for controlling pests of stored products such as grain. The grain would become contaminated with the dead bodies of pest and control agent alike!

Often, neither chemical control nor biological control alone is really effective in controlling pests. Biological control is often enhanced when low levels of pesticides are used at the same time. This is a simple example of an **integrated control system**.

Integrated crop management

This is a more sophisticated approach to optimising crop yield than just using a combination of chemical and biological control. In integrated crop management, most or all of the following would be considered:

- selecting crops that are adapted to the type of soil and climate in the area
- selecting crops that have some resistance to known pests in the area
- choosing appropriate methods of pest control
- rotation of crops grown in a particular field so that the same pests do not build up in the soil and the same ions are not continually removed by the crop
- using fertilisers (organic, inorganic or a combination) that are appropriate to the conditions, to replace the mineral ions removed by cropping
- appropriate treatment and storage of the final crop
- irrigation of the soil (where necessary)

By using a combination of these techniques, a farmer can reduce damage by pests and ensure that crops have a continuous supply of mineral ions.

What the examiners will expect you to be able to do

- Recall any of the key facts.
- Explain any of the key concepts.
- Relate the adaptations of cereals to the conditions in which they are grown.
- Under specified conditions, compare the rates of photosynthesis of maize and sorghum with plants that use normal methods of photosynthesis.
- Interpret graphs showing the effects on the rate of photosynthesis of changing one or more of the factors affecting the process.

- From data supplied, comment on the efficiency of a crop production system and suggest ways to improve it.
- Point out advantages and disadvantages of using organic and inorganic fertilisers.
- From data supplied, suggest the most cost-effective application of a fertiliser (this will be the one that produces the best yield per £1 invested, or per unit of fertiliser applied, and might *not* be the one that produces the greatest yield).
- From data supplied, explain the effects of competition among crop plants and between crop plants and weeds.
- From data supplied, compare the effects of different methods of controlling pests.

Links Much of the material in this unit clearly concerns the application of ecological principles to agriculture. Many of these principles and processes are discussed in detail in Module 5. When you study the biochemistry of photosynthesis, this could easily be related to optimising crop production in glasshouses. Similarly, the study of food chains and energy transfer through ecosystems could be related to bioaccumulation of pesticides along a food chain. The use of fertilisers is easily related to naturally occurring cycles of elements, such as the carbon cycle and the nitrogen cycle.

The control of reproduction in humans and domestic animals

This section considers the hormonal control of reproduction in mammals and some of the ways in which biotechnology allows human fertility to be controlled. The role of biotechnology in controlling reproduction in domestic animals is also considered.

The hormonal control of reproduction in female mammals

Key facts you must know

The ovary of a female mammal contains thousands of **follicles**, each of which contains an **oocyte** (immature egg cell) that may be stimulated by hormones to develop into an **ovum** (mature egg cell).

The release of hormones controlling the development of the follicles (and oocytes) takes place in a cyclical manner in many mammals. In humans this cycle is called the **menstrual cycle**. In other mammals, it is called the **oestrous cycle**.

Four hormones are involved in controlling this cycle. They are **follicle-stimulating hormone (FSH)**, **luteinising hormone (LH)**, **oestrogen** and **progesterone**. The following table shows their site of production, together with their effects in humans.

Hormone	Secreted by	Target	Effect
FSH	Pituitary gland	Cells in follicles	Stimulates development of follicle Stimulates secretion of oestrogen
LH	Pituitary gland	Cells in follicles	Stimulates ovulation, formation of corpus luteum and secretion of progesterone by corpus luteum
Oestrogen	Cells in follicle	Endometrium (lining of uterus) Pituitary gland	Stimulates development of endometrium Inhibits secretion of FSH
Progesterone	Cells in follicle/ corpus luteum	Endometrium Pituitary gland	Maintains and vascularises endometrium Inhibits production of FSH and LH

These changes are summarised in the diagrams below.

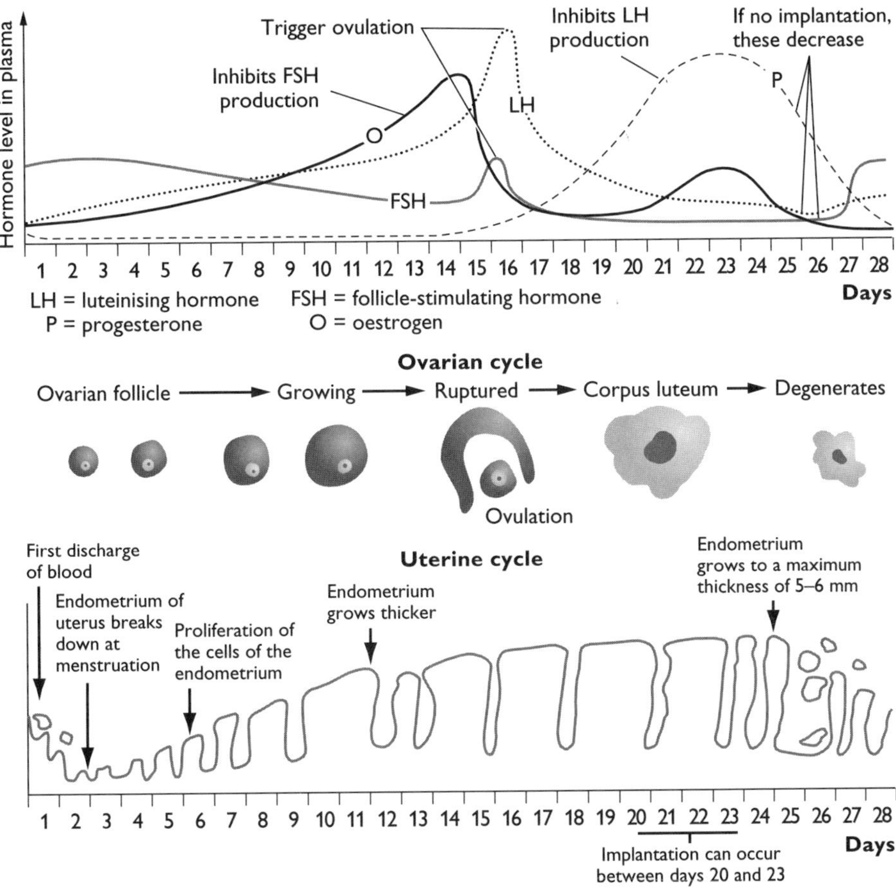

The changes associated with the oestrous cycle in other mammals are similar, but menstruation (breakdown and loss of the endometrium) does not occur.

The length of the oestrus cycle varies. In cows and pigs it is about 21 days and occurs throughout the year. In sheep it is about 16 days, but only takes place during the autumn and early winter months. The period of the cycle during which ovulation occurs is called **oestrus** or **heat** (because of the 1°C rise in body temperature).

Females will only mate during oestrus, which usually lasts for only 1 or 2 days depending on the species.

Key concepts you must understand

The levels of the pituitary hormones are controlled by **negative feedback**. FSH stimulates the secretion of oestrogen by the follicles. As the level of oestrogen rises, it inhibits the secretion of FSH. Similarly, LH stimulates the secretion of progesterone by the corpus luteum. As the level of progesterone rises, the secretion of LH is inhibited. The decrease in levels of the pituitary hormones leads to a decrease in the levels of the ovarian hormones. The low levels of oestrogen and progesterone result in:

- breakdown of the endometrium and menstruation (in humans)
- no inhibition of secretion of the pituitary hormones, so the cycle starts again

In most mammals ovulation occurs towards the end of oestrus. This increases the chance that fertilisation will take place as mating is likely to have occurred as soon as the female became receptive (at the onset of oestrus) and sperm will already be in the female reproductive tract.

Controlling fertility

Key facts you must know

The hormones that control the menstrual cycle can be synthesised in the laboratory or extracted from genetically engineered microorganisms.

These synthetic hormones can be used to control fertility. FSH can be used to increase the number of follicles that develop in a woman who is not ovulating regularly. Oestrogen and progesterone are used in the contraceptive pill to prevent ovulation.

Human female infertility can be treated in the following way:

- FSH is given early in the menstrual cycle — this causes several follicles to develop
- just before the follicles are fully mature, the oocytes are removed
- the oocytes are maintained in a fluid similar to the fluid in the oviducts
- sperm from her partner are added and then the culture is examined for evidence of fertilisation (this is called **in vitro fertilisation (IVF)**)
- once the embryos have developed to the four- or eight-cell stage, two or three are returned to the oviducts in the hope that one might implant in the uterine lining

FSH can also be used in domestic animals to increase the number of follicles that develop. These can then be fertilised by artificial insemination to give large numbers of embryos which can be transplanted into surrogate mothers.

Key concepts you must understand

The success of in vitro fertilisation depends on FSH stimulating the development of follicles. Oestrogen and progesterone inhibit the secretion of FSH. Without FSH, no follicles will develop and pregnancy is not possible. This is the basis of the contraceptive pill.

Embryo transplantation allows large numbers of embryos from a single 'superior' female to be transplanted to surrogates who will carry these until born. The reproductive capacity of the 'superior' animal is increased enormously. The basic procedure in cattle is:

- a 'superior' cow is injected with FSH to induce multiple ovulation
- sperm, which have been selected for sex and for lack of genetic defects, are used to inseminate the cow
- the embryos are recovered and checked for sex and for genetic defects
- selected embryos are split at the eight-cell stage; the resulting cells are allowed to develop so as to increase the number of suitable embryos
- a number of cattle are given injections of progesterone to bring them to the appropriate stage of the oestrous cycle to allow implantation
- the embryos are implanted in the uteri of the recipient cattle

Reproductive hormones can also be used to bring sheep to the same stage of the oestrous cycle. This has the advantage that mating can be better controlled and timed so that most of the lambs are born at an appropriate time of year. The usual method of achieving this is to give all the sheep injections of progesterone for 3 or 4 days. These injections inhibit the release of FSH, whatever the stage of the oestrous cycle. After the injections, the progesterone levels fall, inhibition is removed and *all* the animals start a new oestrous cycle *at the same time*.

Injections of the hormone bovine somatotrophin (BST) can increase milk yields in cattle. The hormone can now be produced by genetically engineered bacteria.

What the examiners will expect you to be able to do

- Recall any of the key facts.
- Explain any of the key principles.
- From data supplied, relate time of insemination of an animal to the likelihood of fertilisation.
- Identify hormones from their effects and from the changes in the level of their secretion throughout the oestrous/menstrual cycle.
- Suggest economic benefits resulting from embryo transfer and oestrus synchronisation.

Links Negative feedback methods for controlling hormone levels feature in later modules. These can clearly be linked to the control of levels of reproductive hormones.

Questions & Answers

This section contains questions similar in style to those you can expect to see in your Unit 2 examination. The limited number of questions means that it is impossible to cover all the topics and all the question styles, but they should give you a flavour of what to expect. The responses that are shown are real students' answers to the questions.

There are several ways of using this section. You could:

- 'hide' the answers to each question and try the question yourself. It needn't be a memory test — use your notes to see if you can actually make all the points you ought to make
- check your answers against the candidates' responses and make an estimate of the likely standard of your response to each question
- check your answers against the examiner's comments to see if you can appreciate where you might have lost marks
- check your answers against the terms used in the question — did you *explain* when you were asked to, or did you merely *describe*?

Examiner's comments

All candidate responses are followed by examiner's comments. These are preceded by the icon e and indicate where credit is due. In the weaker answers, they also point out areas for improvement, specific problems and common errors such as lack of clarity, weak or non-existent development, irrelevance, misinterpretation of the question and mistaken meanings of terms.

The structure of DNA and RNA

(a) Figure 1 represents the structure of the DNA molecule.

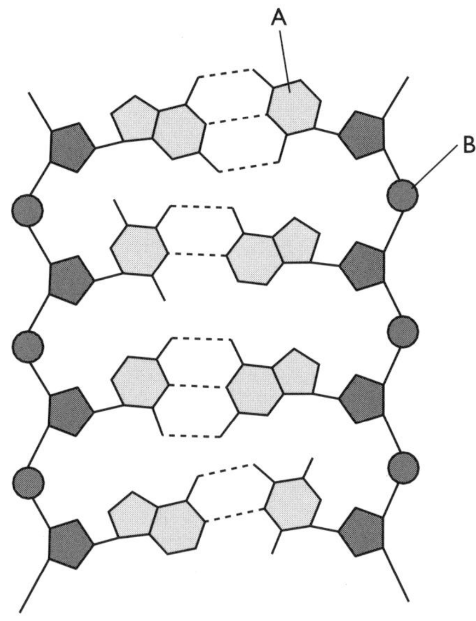

Figure 1

(i) Name the structures labelled A and B. (2 marks)

(ii) Use the diagram to explain why the DNA molecule is sometimes described as consisting of two polynucleotide strands. (1 mark)

(b) Complete the table to show three differences in structure between DNA and mRNA.

DNA	mRNA

(3 marks)

Total: 6 marks

■ ■ ■

Candidates' answers to Question 1

Candidate A

(a) (i) A — nucleotide; B — phosphorus

Candidate B

(a) (i) A is a nitrogenous base (adenine, thymine, cytosine or guanine); B is a phosphate group which links adjacent nucleotides.

question

Candidate A is clearly confused between nucleotide and nitrogenous base — make sure you aren't, it's not a difficult question. Phosphorus is a chemical element and is not an acceptable answer. B is a phosphate group. Candidate B is clearly familiar with the components of a DNA molecule and is awarded both marks.

Candidate A

(a) (ii) There are two strands with lots of nucleotides joined.

Candidate B

(a) (ii) Each strand consists of many nucleotides linked by the phosphate groups. 'Poly-' means many, like in a polygon.

Both candidates clearly understand the idea, for 1 mark.

Candidate A

(b)

DNA	mRNA
is made of two strands	only has one strand
has uracil instead of thymine	has thymine instead of uracil
has a different sugar	has a different sugar

Candidate B

(b) 

DNA	mRNA
DNA is a double helix	RNA is just a single helix
The pentose sugar is deoxyribose	The pentose sugar is ribose
DNA is a much larger molecule	RNA is smaller

Candidate A's answer suggests an understanding of the structures of the two molecules, for 1 mark, but demonstrates a lack of clarity about the facts. There is confusion as to which nucleic acid contains uracil and although the candidate knows that the sugars in the two molecules are different, this is not enough. Contrast this with the precise answers given by Candidate B (full marks). Candidate A's lack of precision is probably a result of insufficiently thorough preparation. Don't leave anything to chance — revise it all.

This is a quite straightforward question with no difficult concepts involved. It is just a matter of knowing the relevant biology. Examiners would expect a grade-A candidate and even a grade-C candidate to score nearly full marks on a question like this. How did you get on?

The use of microbial enzymes in biotechnology

(a) High-fructose corn syrup is used as a sweetener. It is produced from corn starch. The starch grains are ground to a slurry and then enzymes are added, which produce glucose syrup. This is concentrated and decolorised before it is passed through a column of immobilised glucose isomerase. Here, much of the glucose is converted to fructose which is collected and purified. Fructose has the same energy content as glucose, but it is much sweeter.

(i) Complete the flow chart (Figure 1).

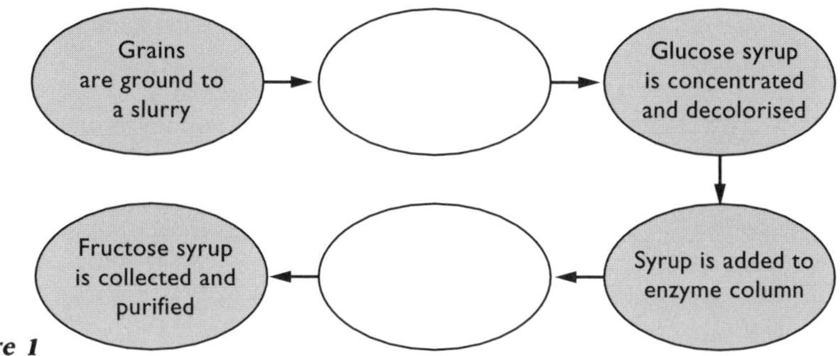

Figure 1 (1 mark)

(ii) Explain two advantages of using immobilised enzymes in this process. (2 marks)

(iii) Explain why fructose is preferred to glucose as a sweetener in the food and drinks industry. (2 marks)

(b) Figure 2 shows an enzyme column which converts glucose into fructose.

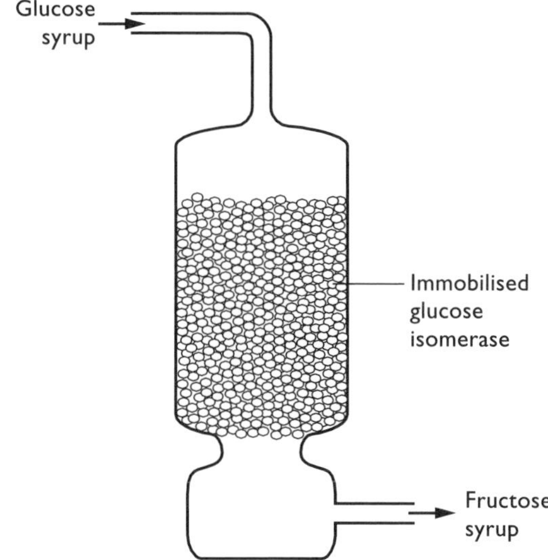

Figure 2

(i) What would be the likely effect on the process of increasing the flow rate of glucose syrup? Explain your answer. (2 marks)

(ii) What term describes the isolation and purification of a product? (1 mark)

Total: 8 marks

Candidates' answers to Question 2

Candidate A

(a) (i)

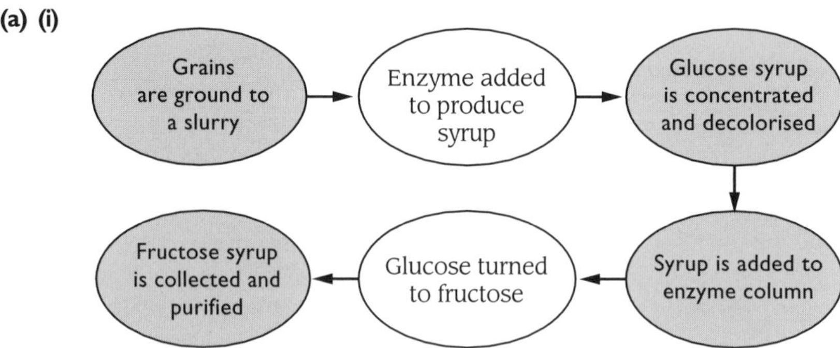

Candidate B

(a) (i)

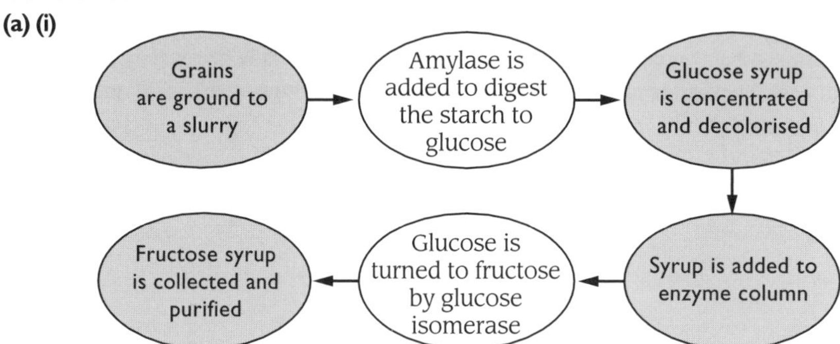

Both candidates have extracted the relevant information from the passage and each is awarded 1 mark. Candidate B has chosen to give extra information by naming the enzyme used in the second stage of the process. This can be a dangerous strategy. If Candidate A had given a wrong enzyme, the mark would have been lost. **If you choose to give more detail than the question demands, you must be absolutely correct.**

Candidate A

(a) (ii) The enzyme can be used again since it is immobilised, and therefore it is cheaper to use. The enzyme stays in the column and so it is cheaper to purify the product.

Candidate B

(a) (ii) The enzyme will not contaminate the product and so downstream processing will be less complicated and so cheaper. It allows the use of continuous production processes. In these, the reactants flow over the enzyme and the reaction can take place for long periods of time without the need to stop the process, extract the product and start all over again. This saves time and money.

e Both candidates have made two valid points and each is awarded 2 marks, but just look at how much Candidate B has written for 2 marks. **Don't include unnecessary detail in your answers — it earns no marks and wastes time.**

Candidate A

(a) (iii) Fructose is sweeter than glucose so glucose would be less efficient.

Candidate B

(a) (iii) Because fructose is sweeter than glucose, less will be needed to produce the same sweetening effect. This has two benefits. Firstly, it will probably be cheaper for the producers and, secondly, it will mean that the product will have less calories and so be healthier.

e Candidate A has selected the appropriate information from the passage, but has merely repeated it and given a vague suggestion that glucose will be less efficient — 0 marks. But less efficient at what — and why? Candidate B has also selected the appropriate information but has explained the possible benefits, for 2 marks.

Candidate A

(b) (i) It would be less efficient, because the syrup would be flowing too fast and would flow by the enzymes without having time to bind to the active sites.

Candidate B

(b) (i) Increasing the flow rate may increase the rate of binding with the enzyme so the reaction would be faster and more fructose syrup would be produced faster.

e Candidate A understands that rate of reaction depends on the rate of binding with the active sites, but somehow thinks that increasing the flow rate (which will make more substrate available per second) will decrease the rate of reaction — 0 marks. Candidate B is able to relate the rate of substrate binding to the situation described, and so is awarded 2 marks.

Candidate A

(b) (ii) Downstream processing

Candidate B

(b) (ii) This is called downstream processing.

e Both candidates score 1 mark.

e **Most of this question is straightforward, and a grade-C candidate should score good marks on most parts. Sections (a) (iii) and (b) (i) require analysis and deduction and the grade-A candidate should score better here.**

Mitosis and meiosis

Figure 1 shows a cell in a stage of mitosis. The cell contains just two pairs of homologous chromosomes.

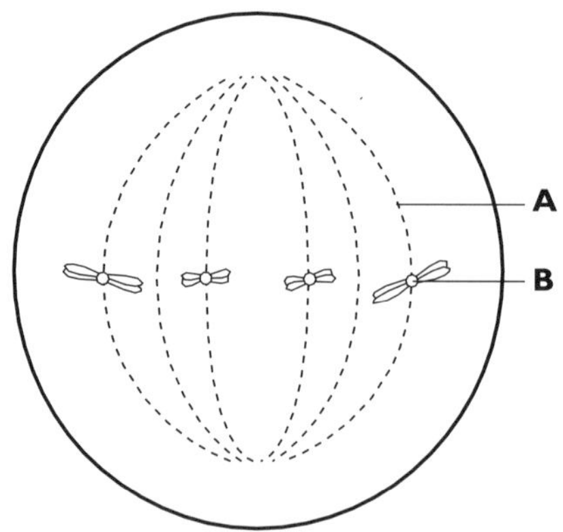

Figure 1

(a) (i) What are *homologous chromosomes*? (1 mark)

(ii) Identify the structures labelled A and B on Figure 1. (2 marks)

(iii) Name the stage of mitosis represented in this diagram. Give a reason for your answer. (1 mark)

Figure 2 shows the life cycle of a mammal.

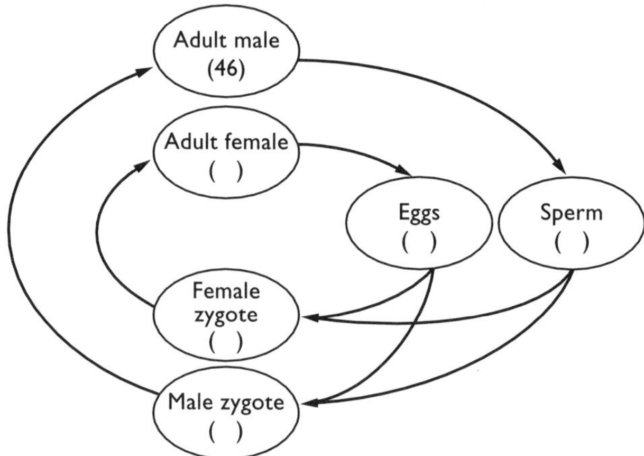

Figure 2

(b) (i) Mark on the diagram *one* stage where meiosis takes place and *one* place where mitosis takes place. (2 marks)

(ii) Complete the empty boxes to show the number of chromosomes per cell. (1 mark)

Total: 7 marks

Candidates' answers to Question 3

Candidate A

(a) (i) They have the same genes.

Candidate B

(a) (i) A homologous pair of chromosomes is a pair of chromosomes that have the same genes along their length (although they may not have the same alleles).

Both candidates score the mark but, again, Candidate B has written much more than is necessary. **Just answer the question, without writing part of it out again.**

Candidate A

(a) (ii) **A** is the spindle; **B** is a chromosome.

Candidate B

(a) (ii) **A** is the spindle or, more accurately, one of the spindle fibres.
B is the centromere, which holds the chromatids in a chromosome together.

Candidate A has not looked carefully enough at label **B** which indicates, precisely, the centromere.

Candidate A

(a) (iii) Prophase

Candidate B

(a) (iii) Metaphase

Candidate A has not revised mitosis effectively. **This is a straightforward piece of biological knowledge which any candidate who has prepared thoroughly should know.**

Candidate A

(b) (i) and (ii)

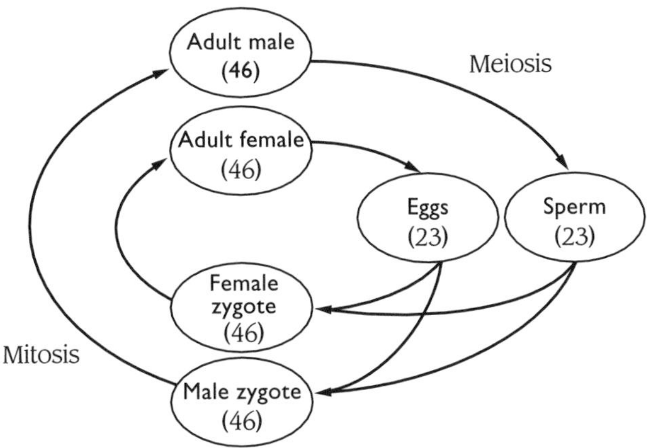

Candidate B

(b) (i) and (ii)

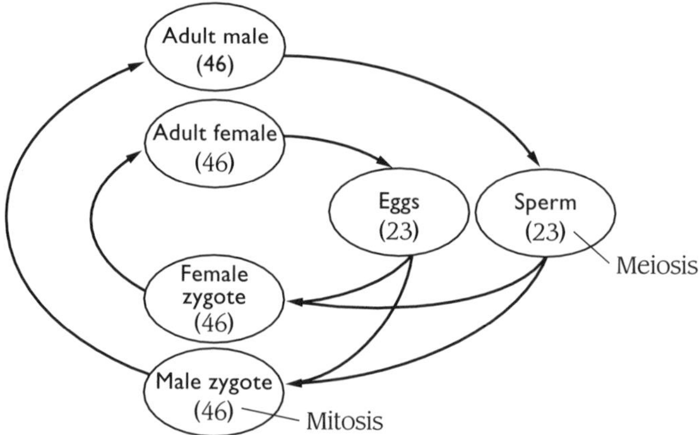

Candidate A is awarded 2 marks for part (b) (i). Candidate B also probably knows exactly where and when the two processes occur, but the labelling is unfortunate. Meiosis does not occur actually *in the sperm*, so this mark is not awarded. However, the zygote does divide by mitosis and so this mark can be awarded. **You will be expected to know that meiosis occurs *only in the formation of gametes* and that all other cell divisions are by mitosis. You should be able to relate this to a life cycle that you have not studied before.** Both candidates understand the halving of chromosomes in the gametes and the restoration of the normal (diploid) number in the zygote. Each is awarded the mark for part (b) (ii).

Most of this question is fairly straightforward biology and examiners would expect both grade-A candidates and grade-C candidates to score well. But remember, they're only easy if you know the answers — so prepare thoroughly.

Protein synthesis

Protein synthesis takes place in the ribosomes. The code for synthesis of a particular protein is specified by a section of the DNA molecule and is carried to the ribosomes by mRNA.

(a) (i) What do we call a section of DNA that codes for a protein? (1 mark)

(ii) The DNA code is sometimes called a *degenerate* code. What does this mean? (2 marks)

(b) Figure 1 shows protein synthesis taking place in a ribosome.

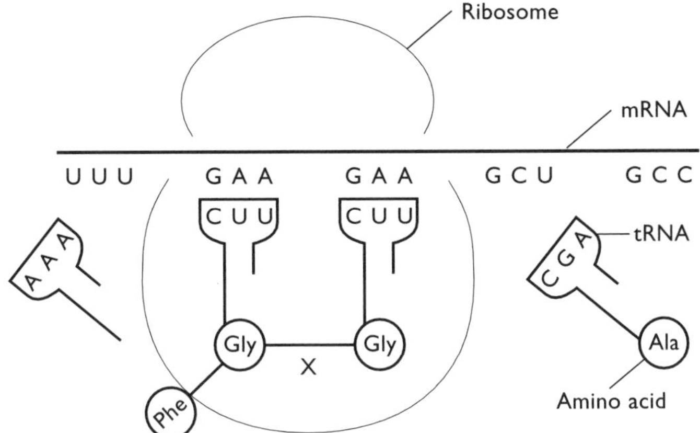

Figure 1

(i) Name the type of bond labelled X. (1 mark)

(ii) Use examples from the diagram to explain the terms *codon* and *anticodon*. (2 marks)

Total: 6 marks

Candidates' answers to Question 4

Candidate A

(a) (i) A gene

Candidate B

(a) (i) A small section of DNA that codes for a protein is called a gene.

e Both candidates know that a gene codes for a protein and each is awarded 1 mark.

Candidate A

(a) (ii) There are more codes than there are amino acids.

Candidate B

(a) (ii) Not all the triplet codes of the DNA code for amino acids. Some are stop codes.

Neither candidate completely answers the question. Each is awarded 1 mark for their correct statement. If they had each included the statement made by the other or had included the idea that some amino acids have more than one code, they would have scored both marks.

Candidate A

(b) (i) Glycosidic

Candidate B

(b) (i) Glycosidic bond

Bonds between amino acids are **peptide bonds**. Both candidates appear to have been confused by the label 'gly' in the diagram. The key makes it quite clear that this is an abbreviation for the amino acid glycine. **Look carefully at all the information you are given in a question.**

Candidate A

(b) (ii) GAA is a codon; CUU is an anticodon

Candidate B

(b) (ii) A codon is a triplet of bases on the mRNA molecule — such as GAA. An anticodon is a triplet of bases on the tRNA molecule.

Neither candidate really makes both points here. Candidate A is awarded 1 mark as (in this instance) the examples chosen can only be codon and anticodon respectively and also *they are complementary* — but is this good luck or does the candidate really understand that codon and anticodon must be complementary? Candidate B is not awarded any marks, despite probably understanding the concepts quite well. There is no example of an anticodon and there is no indication that codon and anticodon are complementary or that they code for an amino acid. **The examiner will not assume *anything* for you: you must explain *everything*.**

This is a topic that many candidates find difficult, as it pulls together knowledge from a number of areas. However, much of it depends only on learning the relevant facts.

Immunity

Part of our immune response involves the production of antibodies in response to specific foreign antigens. Figure 1 shows the levels of the antibody response to two injections of the same antigen.

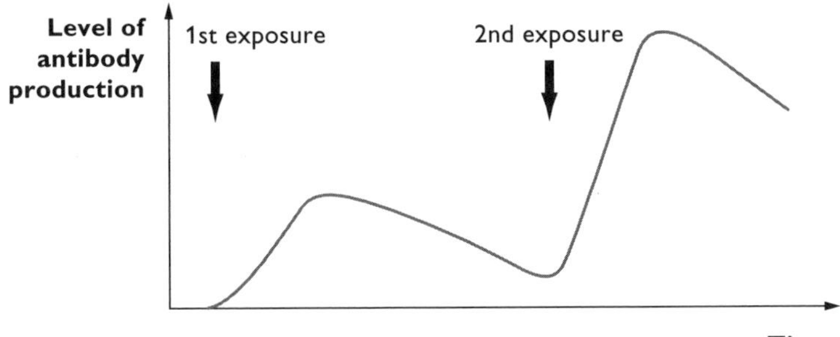

Figure 1

(a) (i) What is an antigen? (1 mark)

(ii) Describe two differences between the responses to the first and second injections of the antigen. (2 marks)

(b) Explain how we become immune to a disease following exposure to the microorganism causing the disease. (3 marks)

Total: 6 marks

Candidates' answers to Question 5

Candidate A

(a) (i) An antigen is something that shouldn't be in your body.

Candidate B

(a) (i) An antigen is a foreign substance — often a foreign glycoprotein on the surface of a cell.

e A spanner shouldn't be in your body — but it is not an antigen. Candidate A's answer is totally inadequate, although he or she may well have known more and, if someone had said 'be more precise', may well have done so. Candidate B clearly understands what an antigen is — although it needn't be foreign. You have your own 'set' of antigens on your cells.

Candidate A

(a) (ii) The first response produces more antibody and it drops to a lower level.

Candidate B

(a) (ii) The second response is quicker and produces more antibody than the first.

Candidate A's answer is wrong — 0 marks. Candidate B has noticed the difference in gradient as well as the difference in amount produced, and is awarded both marks. **Look carefully at all aspects of graphs. Differences in gradient can indicate differences in rate.**

Candidate A

(b) Lymphocytes in our blood system produce antibodies which destroy the microorganisms that have infected us. Some of the lymphocytes become memory cells which stay in our body and can fight off future infections.

Candidate B

(b) When a microorganism enters our body, B lymphocytes are stimulated to produce specific antibodies against the antigens on the microorganisms. They multiply and eventually destroy all the microorganisms. Some of the lymphocytes become memory cells and remain in our bodies. If we are infected again by the same microorganism, these memory cells can destroy it quickly.

Both candidates seem to understand what happens, but neither has supplied sufficient detail. Examiners would hope to see a mention of B lymphocytes multiplying and producing *specific* antibodies. Some of these would become memory cells and remain in our bodies and, upon re-infection, would be able to destroy the microorganisms quickly *because they are present in much larger numbers than at the initial infection*. Candidate A scores 1 mark and Candidate B 2 marks.

Marks can be easily lost on an apparently straightforward question like this by not looking carefully enough at, and not using, all the information supplied. When you have to write more than just a line or two for an answer, read through it and ask yourself 'So what?'. If you can find an answer to the 'So what?', you probably need to include it!

Crop production (I)

Organisms that reduce the yield of a crop plant are called pests. They can be controlled using pesticides, by biological control or by integrated crop management.

Figure 1 shows the effects of repeated pesticide applications on a population of pests.

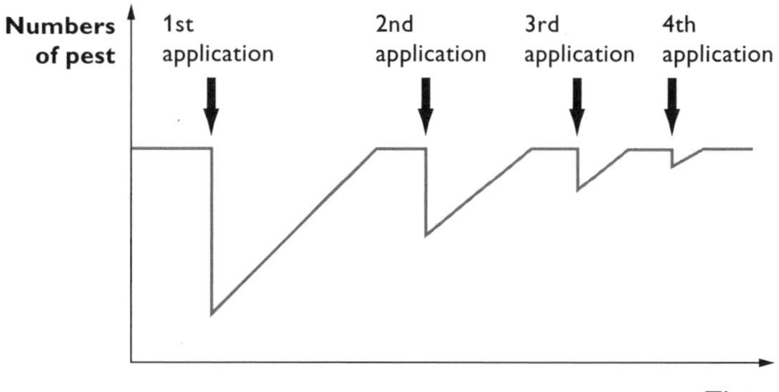

(a) (i) Suggest two reasons why the first application of the pesticide does not reduce the pest population to zero. (2 marks)

(ii) Explain the reduction in effect of the pesticide at the second, third and fourth applications. (3 marks)

(b) Give one benefit of each of the following in an integrated crop management system:

(i) crop rotation (not growing the same crop in the same field in successive years)

(ii) using organic fertilisers (such as farmyard manure) rather than inorganic fertilisers

(iii) planting crops that are tolerant of the local soil pH conditions (3 marks)

Total: 8 marks

■ ■ ■

Candidates' answers to Question 6

Candidate A

(a) (i) The dose might not have been strong enough and some of them might not have been affected by it.

Candidate B

(a) (i) Some of the pests might have a mutation that gives them resistance to the pesticide. Insecticides are usually sprayed and not all the pests are 'hit'.

e What does Candidate A mean by 'not strong enough' and 'not affected by it'? Probably that the concentration of the insecticide wasn't strong enough to be toxic in some cases and that some of the pests were resistant. But this is not what the

question

examiner is reading. Candidate A is awarded 1 mark — 'not strong enough' is really too vague, but 'may not be affected by it' does seem to convey the idea of resistance. This is only *my* opinion — another examiner might decide that both are too vague and award no marks. Candidate B clearly makes two valid points and is awarded 2 marks. **Learn, and try to use, the appropriate biological terms.**

Candidate A

(a) (ii) More of the pests become immune to the pesticide. These survive and those that aren't immune are killed and so there are less of them.

Candidate B

(a) (ii) Some of the pests are resistant and these survive the initial application. These reproduce so that when the insecticide is re-applied, fewer of the pests are killed.

e Neither candidate has offered a really full explanation, although both seem to understand the ideas. Candidate A talks about immunity, which is wrong — you become immune to antigens, not pesticides. There is a hint, however, that as time goes by, there will be more of the resistant forms in the population and less of the non-resistant forms. Candidate A scores just 1 mark. Candidate B makes two points clearly — the difference in survival between resistant and non-resistant forms and that this will lead to more resistant forms reproducing compared with non-resistant forms. This is repeated with each application (a point which neither makes) and, each time, the proportion of resistant forms in the population increases. Candidate B scores 2 marks.

Candidate A

(b) (i) Insect pests won't have the same crops to feed on and so they die out.

Candidate B

(b) (i) The pests probably feed mainly on one crop plant, so by changing the crop every year you don't get a build up of any one pest. It might not kill them off though.

e Both candidates appear to understand the effects of crop rotation. Each scores 1 mark.

Candidate A

(b) (ii) To supply what the plant needs in a natural form.

Candidate B

(b) (ii) Organic fertilisers don't supply all the minerals all at once; they release them slowly, like a 'drip-feed'.

e Candidate A's answer is a good example of the sort of thing you should *never* write. It conveys about as much biological information as saying vegetables have a lot of 'goodness' in them. What on earth does goodness mean? **Be precise and be accurate.** Candidate B has the right idea, for 1 mark.

Candidate A

(b) (iii) If they weren't from the area, and the soil was too acid, they might not grow properly.

Candidate B

(b) (iii) They will be able to compete effectively with any local weeds, which will also be adapted to the conditions.

e Both candidates clearly understand the benefit and are awarded 1 mark.

e **Much of this question is relatively straightforward and examiners would expect a grade-C candidate to score approximately 4 or 5 of the 7 marks available. A grade-A candidate should do even better. The hardest part of this question is part (a) (ii), where clear explanation is required. Make sure that you write clearly in such situations. If you find it easier to write a series of bullet-pointed statements as an explanation, then do so.**

The polymerase chain reaction

The polymerase chain reaction (PCR) is a method of obtaining large amounts of DNA from a small initial sample. Figure 1 shows the main stages in the polymerase chain reaction.

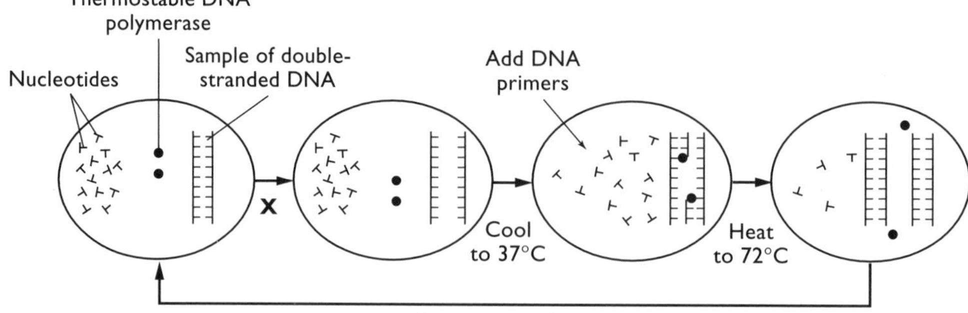

Figure 1

(a) (i) What must be done to separate the strands of DNA (process X)? (1 mark)

(ii) What are primers? (2 marks)

(b) (i) What is meant by 'thermostable DNA polymerase'? (2 marks)

(ii) What is the main advantage of using a thermostable DNA polymerase in this process? (1 mark)

Total: 6 marks

■ ■ ■

Candidates' answers to Question 7

Candidate A

(a) (i) You must heat them.

Candidate B

(a) (i) The DNA must be heated to 95°C to separate the strands.

> Both candidates score the mark here. There is no need to know the precise temperature — you are sitting a biology examination, not one in production engineering!

Candidate A

(a) (ii) Primers are small sections of DNA that start the new strands.

Candidate B

(a) (ii) Primers are small sections of single-stranded DNA which are complementary to one end of the original DNA strands.

> Candidate A clearly understands what primers do and, to an extent, what primers are. However, the key point that they are single-stranded is missing. Double-

stranded DNA could not bind to the original strands in the way the primers do. Candidate A scores 1 mark. Candidate B knows that the primers are single-stranded and that their base sequences are complementary to those on the original strands. Although there is no mention of function, there is still enough information here to score 2 marks.

Candidate A

(b) (i) A thermostable DNA polymerase is one that is not easily denatured at high temperatures.

Candidate B

(b) (i) A thermostable DNA polymerase has a tertiary structure which is more stable and less easily deformed by heat.

e Both candidates have explained 'thermostable' well — but neither has described what is meant by 'DNA polymerase' which is also included in the terms to be explained. Each scores 1 mark. **Read the question carefully and make sure that you explain everything required. If a phrase is enclosed in quotes, make sure that you explain everything within the quotes.**

Candidate A

(b) (ii) You can make the reaction faster by having it hotter.

Candidate B

(b) (ii) The enzyme will still be active at high temperatures. Probably its optimum is high — it isn't easily denatured because of the strong bonds holding its tertiary structure.

e Candidate A has explained the benefit — just, for 1 mark. A faster reaction means more product per minute for a manufacturer. Candidate B has really only explained again (and in some detail) what thermostable means, and gets no marks. There is no description of an *advantage*. **Another instance of not applying the 'so what?' test.**

e **Another question which is 'easy if you know the answers'. There are no difficult ideas and no complex data. So, did *you* know the answers?**

Using biotechnology in forensic science

Genetic fingerprinting involves the analysis of sections of non-coding DNA. Unlike blood grouping, which can only ever prove the innocence of a suspect, genetic fingerprinting can establish guilt with a high degree of certainty.

(a) (i) What is meant by non-coding DNA? (1 mark)

(ii) Explain why only non-coding DNA is used in genetic fingerprinting? (2 marks)

(iii) Why can blood grouping alone not establish the guilt of a suspect? (1 mark)

(b) Three suspects were tested to see what blood group each was. The results of the tests are shown in Figure 1. The blood found at the scene of the crime was blood group A.

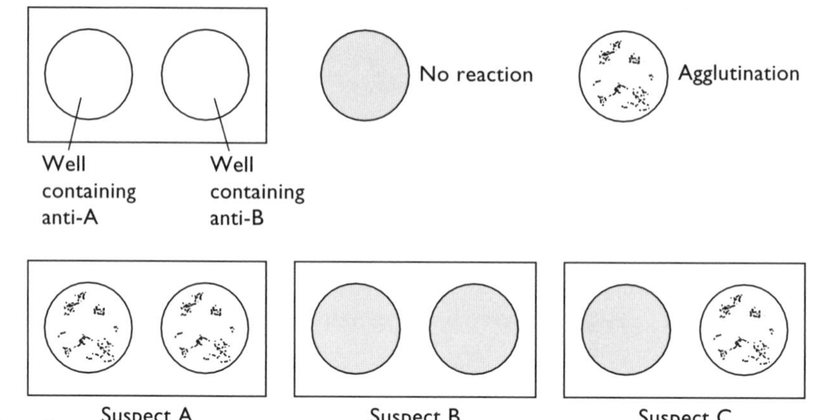

Figure 1

(i) Which of the three suspects should the police eliminate from their enquiries? (1 mark)

(ii) Explain the result obtained for suspect A. (2 marks)

Total: 7 marks

■ ■ ■

Candidates' answers to Question 8

Candidate A

(a) (i) It doesn't code for proteins.

Candidate B

(a) (i) Non-coding DNA is made up of repeated sequences of DNA that don't code for a protein.

e Both candidates score the mark.

Candidate A

(a) (ii) Non-coding DNA differs among different people but coding DNA is the same.

Candidate B

(a) (ii) The non-coding DNA varies between individuals, but the coding DNA codes for proteins, so a lot of it will be the same. The same protein will have the same base sequence coding for it. We all have haemoglobin and the DNA sequence for haemoglobin will be the same in each of us.

e For 1 mark, both candidates realise the basis for using non-coding DNA — it varies between individuals. Only Candidate B explains why it varies, for the second mark. The example of haemoglobin used to illustrate the answer is a little unfortunate as there are mutant alleles which code for abnormal haemoglobin. **Take note of the mark allocation — 2 marks means you must give two separate ideas.**

Candidate A

(a) (iii) Lots of people have the same blood group.

Candidate B

(a) (iii) About 40% of the UK population are blood group A. Identifying a blood group just puts them in the frame along with the 20 million others.

e Both candidates score the mark but Candidate B has supplied more than was needed.

Candidate A

(b) (i) Suspects A and B.

Candidate B

(b) (i) All of them: Suspect A is blood group AB, Suspect B is blood group O and Suspect C is blood group B. Since the blood group at the scene of the crime was blood group A, none of them can have committed the crime.

e Candidate B has deduced the answer correctly but has again written far more than necessary. No explanation was asked for.

Candidate A

(b) (ii) Suspect A is blood group AB and so his/her blood reacts with both antibodies.

Candidate B

(b) (ii) Suspect A is blood group AB as there has been a reaction with both antibodies. So he must be blood group AB.

e Neither candidate explains *why* the suspect's blood reacts with both antibodies, and both lose 1 mark. There is a step missing in their logic. They jump straight from saying that the blood reacts with both antibodies (no mark for this as it is shown in the diagram) to saying that the suspect must be blood group AB, with no mention of the antigens.

e **There are a number of instances in this question where precise answers are required. Producing these is more difficult as you are often being asked to process the information before you can formulate an answer. A vague idea is not good enough.**

Crop production (II)

Rice and maize are cereals. They form an important part of the diet of the people in the regions of the world where they are cultivated.

(a) Rice is cultivated in 'paddy fields' in many eastern countries. The crop is grown in fields which frequently become flooded and parts, or sometimes all, of the crop become submerged.

(i) Explain how the rice crop is able to survive periods of total submergence. (2 marks)

(ii) Give two other features of rice which allow it to grow effectively in the paddy fields. (2 marks)

(b) Maize has a specialised method of photosynthesis which is more efficient than the normal method of photosynthesis at high temperatures and low carbon dioxide concentrations. Figure 1 shows the effect of differing carbon dioxide concentrations on the rate of photosynthesis in plants that use the normal method of photosynthesis.

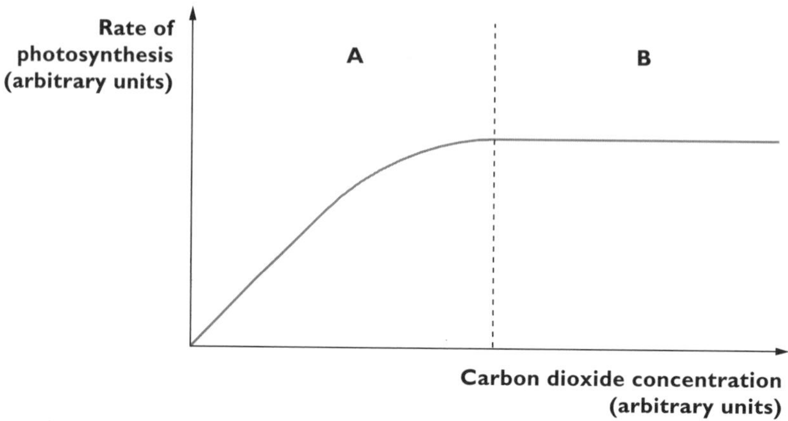

Figure 1

(i) Suggest two reasons why the rate of photosynthesis remains constant in region B. Give an explanation for each reason you suggest. (4 marks)

(ii) Sketch, on the graph, the curve you would expect if the same experiment had been carried out using either sorghum or maize. (1 mark)

(c) Some strains of maize have been genetically engineered to make them resistant to the 'corn borer', an insect that causes serious damage to maize crops. The gene introduced comes from a bacterium and codes for a protein toxic to the insect. Other strains of maize have been engineered to make them tolerant to herbicides. Suggest how combining these two traits in one strain of maize could eventually result in improved crop yields as well as reduced costs for the grower. (6 marks)

Total: 15 marks

Candidates' answers to Question 9

Candidate A

(a) (i) It can get oxygen from the spaces in the stem or just respire anaerobically.

Candidate B

(a) (i) It can respire anaerobically for a long time and tolerate the ethanol that is produced.

Both candidates appreciate that if the plant is totally submerged, then it must respire anaerobically, for the first mark, although Candidate A seems to think that there may still be some oxygen available. Candidate B is also aware of the ethanol tolerance shown by rice, which is the true adaptation, and is awarded the second mark.

Candidate A

(a) (ii) It has hollow stems with air in it and can survive when ethanol has been produced.

Candidate B

(a) (ii) Rice has stems with aerenchyma which allows the rapid diffusion of oxygen from aerial parts to submerged parts. It also has extra roots growing from nodes on the stem. This allows extra uptake of minerals from the water.

Both know that the aerenchyma is an adaptation and Candidate B is also aware of the nodal roots and so is awarded 2 marks, while Candidate A only scores 1. But Candidate B has done more than the examiner intended. The candidate has also included explanations that were not asked for and will earn no extra marks. **Read the question carefully, and if you are not asked to explain, don't use up valuable time doing so.**

Candidate A

(b) (i) There is not enough light. Light is needed to provide the energy. Also, it is probably not warm enough. Photosynthesis works better when it is warmer.

Candidate B

(b) (i) In region B, carbon dioxide is non-limiting, so some other factor must be limiting the rate of photosynthesis. This could be either insufficient light or insufficient heat.

Candidate A has suggested two environmental factors which could be limiting the rate of photosynthesis. The explanation for light (that it supplies the energy for the process) is adequate, but just to say that photosynthesis 'works better when it is warmer' is hardly an explanation. Candidate A scores 3 marks. Candidate B seems to think that mentioning that carbon dioxide is non-limiting has explained how insufficient light and heat limit the rate of photosynthesis. This is not enough and scores only 2 marks. **When you are giving reasons for a deduction, make sure that your reasons can link the deduction directly to the data.**

Candidate A

(b) (ii)

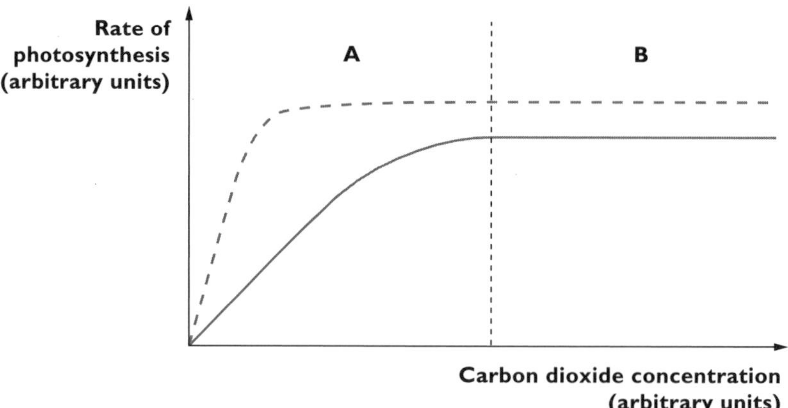

Candidate B

(b) (ii)

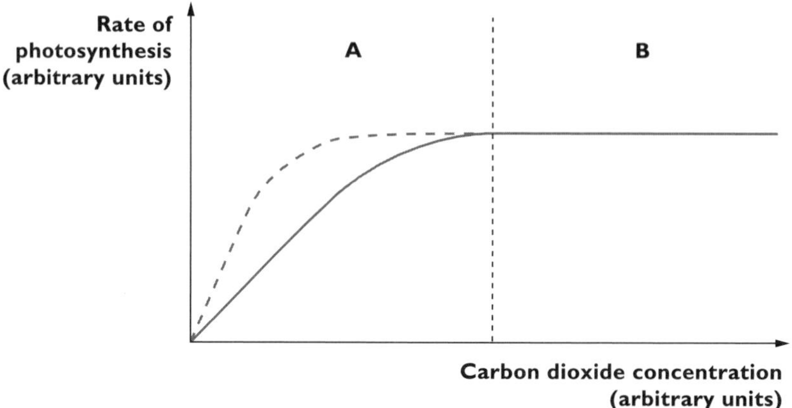

e Maize and sorghum only photosynthesise more efficiently at low carbon dioxide concentrations. Candidate B shows this clearly in the graph while Candidate A's graph suggests that they are more efficient at all concentrations. Did Candidate A take note of all the information supplied? Make sure that you do.

Candidate A

(c) The maize will have its own internal insecticide in the toxic protein, so the grower will not have to spend money on spraying insecticide. If the crop doesn't get damaged by the insects, there will be a bigger yield to sell. The grower will have to spend money on the herbicides, but these won't affect the crop. If the weeds are all killed, the maize can use all the water in the soil. The young maize plants won't get choked by weeds.

Candidate B

(c) The insect pests damage the corn and so reduce the yield from the crop. Weeds compete with the corn for water and mineral ions from the soil as well as sunlight and carbon dioxide. This also results in reduced yields and reduced profits for the grower. By using the new genetically modified corn, the grower has a crop which is resistant to the pests. In effect, it has its own pesticide 'built in' and so the corn borer cannot damage the corn and cannot reduce the yield. By also engineering the corn to be tolerant of herbicides, these can be sprayed whenever necessary to control weeds. This allows the corn to obtain more of the mineral ions and water and so improves the yield. Costs have been reduced as there is no need to use (and so no need to purchase) insecticides. However, I do not think that we should use genetically modified crops. They contain new genes which may 'jump' into other species which could also become resistant to herbicides. By genetically modifying plants, scientists are altering nature and changing species forever.

Both these answers demonstrate a clear understanding of the benefits of the genetic modification of the corn and both would be awarded 6 marks. For a question like this, the examiner probably has a list of about eight or nine acceptable points and any six will get you full marks. The relevant points for this particular question would be:

- the toxic protein kills the insects
- there is no need to use insecticides
- there is therefore less expense (no need to buy insecticides)
- there is less damage to crops
- herbicides can be used without damaging the maize at times when they will be most effective
- this may result in less being used over a growing season
- weeds will be controlled effectively
- there is less competition with weeds for carbon dioxide/light/mineral ions/water, so there is a higher yield

Both candidates have clearly made at least six of these points but Candidate A has done it much more succinctly. Candidate B has also offered an opinion on the ethics of using GM crops — which wasn't asked for. **Don't go beyond what the question asks you to do — it will cost you time.**

Although this is a long question, most of the sections just demand recall of key facts or concepts. Only in part (b) do you have to interpret data. In part (c) you must explain the benefits of genetically engineering crops, but all the necessary information is supplied. Examiners would expect grade-A and grade-C candidates alike to perform quite well on a question of this nature.

Control of reproduction

Read the passage below and answer the questions that follow.

Biotechnology is being used in a number of ways to increase the milk yield of cattle. It has been possible for some time now to genetically engineer bacteria to produce the hormone bovine somatotrophin (BST). The gene coding for the production of BST is transferred to bacteria which are then cultured in a large-scale fermenter. The BST they produce is the same as the BST produced by the cattle and acts in the same way — by diverting glucose, fatty acids and body fats to the mammary glands and away from other regions of the body.

More recently it has become possible to produce large numbers of cattle with a high milk yield by the technique of embryo transplantation. Sperm from an 'excellent' bull of the same breed as the cattle are used to fertilise several eggs from one high-yielding cow which has been injected with a hormone to cause multiple ovulation. The resulting embryos are implanted into the uteri of other cattle which have been prepared for pregnancy by injections of other hormones.

(a) (i) Why is the bovine somatotrophin produced by the bacteria identical to that produced by the cattle? (1 mark)

(ii) Explain how injecting cattle with BST could improve their milk yield. (2 marks)

(iii) Describe a likely procedure for transferring the gene coding for the production of BST from cattle cells into bacterial cells. (6 marks)

(b) (i) Injections of which hormone would cause multiple ovulation? Explain how this would happen. (2 marks)

(ii) Name one of the 'other hormones' which are used to prepare the uterus for pregnancy. Explain how the hormone would act. (2 marks)

(iii) Although the bull and the cow are chosen carefully to produce the desired high yield, there can still be considerable variation in the milk yield of the offspring. Explain why. (2 marks)

Total: 15 marks

■ ■ ■

Candidates' answers to Question 10

Candidate A

(a) (i) Because it's made using the same gene.

Candidate B

(a) (i) Both BSTs are identical because the allele which codes for them is the same — the allele has been removed from the cow cell and put into the bacterial cell.

e Clearly, both candidates understand the concept.

Candidate A

(a) (ii) More of the material needed to make milk goes to the mammary glands, so they make more milk.

Candidate B

(a) (ii) BST diverts more nutrients such as glucose, fatty acids and body fats away from other parts of the body and to the mammary glands. These are needed in the formation of milk and so more milk can be produced.

e It is clear that both understand the process, but only Candidate B has given the level of detail required for full marks. 2 marks are allocated and so just writing about 'materials needed', as Candidate A did (0 marks), would not be enough when the actual nutrients are named in the passage. Also, there is no mention of why there are more materials going to the mammary glands, although the information is clearly given in the passage. **Take note of the mark allocations — they can indicate the level of detail needed in your answers.**

Candidate A

(a) (iii) The gene has to be cut out using an enzyme — like molecular scissors. After it has been cut out, the gene has to be put in a vector to carry the gene into the bacteria. Another enzyme is used to join the new gene to the bacteria. To find out which cells have the new gene, the bacteria are grown on an agar gel which contains an antibiotic. Those that grow have the new gene.

Candidate B

(a) (iii) The gene is cut out of the cow cell DNA using a restriction enzyme. Or it could be made using reverse transcriptase. After that, the gene is mixed with plasmids from bacteria. The plasmids are little circles of DNA which have been opened up using the same restriction enzyme. This leaves them with sticky ends so that when the gene is mixed with the plasmid, they will join up. The plasmids are then incubated with bacteria which take them up.

e The specification requires you to know the enzymes used in genetic engineering and to know that plasmids are the most usual vectors for transferring genes into bacterial cells. All of Candidate A's answer is too vague. No specific enzymes are mentioned and, although the concept of a vector is understood, the candidate does not name it as a plasmid. The 'other enzyme' (ligase) 'joins' the gene to a plasmid — not to a bacterium. The only relevant and sufficiently precise point concerns the agar gel containing antibiotic. Candidate A therefore scores only 1 mark. Candidate B gives a more precise and detailed response but also does not mention ligase and this time does not mention the use of antibiotics to check the uptake of plasmids. Still, Candidate B is awarded 5 marks.

Candidate A

(b) (i) Oestrogen, because it's produced by developing follicles.

Candidate B

(b) (i) LH, because it stimulates the rupture of the follicles.

e Candidate A clearly does not understand the relationship between hormones and follicle development and Candidate B has become distracted by the term 'ovulation'. An increase in LH during the oestrus cycle does cause ovulation, but

the follicles must be there in the first place. This is controlled by FSH and it is this hormone which is injected.

Candidate A

(b) (ii) Progesterone is used because it prevents menstruation.

Candidate B

(b) (ii) Progesterone is used because it increases the blood supply to the uterus lining.

e Both have correctly suggested progesterone as the hormone, but neither appears to understand why, so each scores 1 mark. Progesterone inhibits the secretion of FSH. After several daily injections of progesterone, the level of progesterone is allowed to fall which removes the inhibition of FSH and the animals start a new oestrus cycle.

Candidate A

(b) (iii) This could be due to diet. If the offspring do not get the proper balance of nutrients, they will not produce all the milk they could.

Candidate B

(b) (iii) The sperm and egg cells are made by meiosis so there will be variation in these and variation in the zygotes produced by fertilisation. This could affect the milk yield.

e The clue to the desired answer was in the phrase 'variation in milk yield'. It seems unlikely that a farmer, after going to all the expense of artificial insemination, would not then supply a balanced diet. Variation in the sex cells could account for variation in milk yield. Candidate B scores 2 marks, while Candidate A scores none.

e **Part (a) of this question is relatively straightforward. There is a section worth 6 marks, but this simply requires you to describe the basic techniques of gene transfer. Part (b) demands more of you, in that you must apply ideas and deduce answers from information given. Examiners may not expect quite the same level of performance on a long question of this nature. Nevertheless, there is no real excuse for Candidate A scoring only 4 marks in total. You must make sure that you are in a position to score good marks on any question that demands only the recall of facts or concepts.**

Examiner's overview

e **There are 84 marks available in this selection of questions. The module test will be shorter (although there will still be the two long questions at the end) and will amount to only 75 marks.**

Candidate B scores 68 of the 84 marks available, the work of a good grade-A candidate. You would probably get a grade A with fewer marks than this.

Candidate A scores 41 of the 84 marks, probably just enough for a grade C to be awarded. There are two important points about this candidate's work.

(1) The candidate does not perform evenly throughout the test: some questions are answered well, others poorly. For example, 11 out of 15 marks were scored on question 9 while only 4 out of 15 marks were scored on question 10. This suggests gaps in knowledge and understanding which could be due to insufficient preparation.

(2) The candidate could have scored another 8 marks without knowing any more biology, just by being careful:

- **in question 2(a)(iii), the candidate just described glucose as being 'less efficient' without saying in what way — although there is probably little doubt that the candidate knew (2 marks lost)**
- **in question 3(a)(ii), the candidate did not look at label line B carefully enough (1 mark lost)**
- **in question 5(a)(ii), the candidate described the first antibody response as higher; it is obviously the second and the candidate should not have missed this (1 mark lost)**
- **in question 6(a)(i), the candidate did not use precise enough language (1 mark lost)**
- **in question 6(a)(ii), the candidate used an inappropriate biological term and a little more thought would have made it obvious that it was the wrong term (1 mark lost)**
- **in question 10(a)(ii), the candidate found the relevant information in the passage, but then chose to use only part of it and rephrased this in a manner that was much too vague (2 marks lost)**

These extra 8 marks would have raised the grade to a probable B. In addition, there were another 6 marks that were missed because the candidate 'almost knew' the answer. Perhaps one more run through of the notes and the following points would have been scored:

- **in question 1(b) the candidate knows that DNA and mRNA contain different sugars, but can't quite remember what they are (1 mark lost)**
- **in question 5(b) the candidate seems to know how an immune response is produced, but does not remember that it is the B lymphocytes which are involved in antibody production and that *specific* antibodies are produced (2 marks lost)**
- **in question 10(a)(iii), the candidate seems to understand the principles involved in gene transfer, but does not know the names of specific enzymes involved, and has forgotten that plasmids are used to transfer the genes (3 marks lost)**

Altogether, this grade-C candidate could have quite easily scored another 14 marks, taking the total to 55 marks out of 84. This would be close to the mark required for a grade A. Would you be content with a grade C when you could get a grade A? The message is simple: prepare thoroughly and be careful in the examination.